PR
5837
C5
1816

CONTENTS.

The City of the Plague..........................Page 3

Miscellaneous Poems.

The Children's Dance..........................171
Address to a Wild Deer........................188
The Voice of Departed Friendship.............197
Lord Ronald's Child...........................200
The Widow.....................................207
Solitude......................................213
Bessy Bell and Mary Gray......................216
The Scholar's Funeral.........................223
The Convict...................................241
The Sisters...................................292
The Farewell and Return.......................295

THE
CITY OF THE PLAGUE.

THE
CITY OF THE PLAGUE.

ACT I.

SCENE I.

Time, the Afternoon.—Two Naval Officers walking along the banks of the Thames.—They sit down on a stone seat fronting the river.

Frankfort. My heart feels heavier every step I take
Towards the city. Oh! that I could drop
Down like a bird upon its nest, at once
Into my mother's house. There might my soul
Find peace, even 'mid the silent emptiness
That told me she had perish'd.

Wilmot. All around
Appears so bright, so tranquil, and so calm,
That happy omens rise on every side,
To strengthen and support us in our fears.

Frank. Oh Wilmot! to my soul a field of graves,
A church-yard filled with marble monuments,

Profoundly hush'd in death's own sanctity,
Seems not more alien to the voice of Hope
Than that wide wilderness of domes and spires,
Hanging o'er the breathless city.

 Wil.   See! my friend,
How bright the sunshine dances in its joy
O'er the still flow of this majestic river.
I know not how, but, gazing on that light
So beautiful, all images of death
Fade from my roused soul, and I believe
That our journey here must end in happiness.

 Frank. Is it the hour of prayer?

 Wil.   The evening service,
Methinks, must now be closed.

 Frank.   There comes no sound
Of organ-peal or choral symphony
From yonder vast cathedral. How it stands
Amid the silent houses, with a strange
Deep silence of its own! I could believe
That many a Sabbath had pass'd prayerless on
Within its holy solitude. No knee
This day, methinks, hath bent before its altar.

 Wil. It is a solemn pile! yet to mine eye
There rests above its massive sanctity
The clear blue air of peace.

 Frank.   A solemn pile!
Aye! there it stands, like a majestic ruin,
Mouldering in a desert; in whose silent heart

No sound hath leave to dwell. I knew it once,
When music in that chosen temple rais'd
Th' adoring soul to Heaven. But one dread year
Hath done the work of ages; and the Plague
Mocks in his fury the slow hand of time.
  Wil. The sun smiles on its walls.
  Frank.   Why does the finger,
Yellow 'mid the sunshine on the Minster-clock,
Point at that hour? It is most horrible,
Speaking of midnight in the face of day.
During the very dead of night it stopp'd,
Even at the moment when a hundred hearts
Paus'd with it suddenly, to beat no more.
Yet, wherefore should it run its idle round?
There is no need that men should count the hours
Of time, thus standing on eternity.
It is a death-like image.
  Wil.   I could smile
At such fantastic terrors.
  Frank.   How can I,
When round me silent Nature speaks of death,
Withstand such monitory impulses?
When yet far off I thought upon the plague,
Sometimes my mother's image struck my soul
In unchang'd meekness and serenity,
And all my fears were gone. But these green banks,
With an unwonted flush of flowers overgrown,
Brown, when I left them last, with frequent feet,

From morn till evening, hurrying to and fro,
In mournful beauty seem encompassing
A still forsaken city of the dead.
   Wil. It is the Sabbath-day—the day of rest.
   Frank. O unrejoicing Sabbath! not of yore
Did thy sweet evenings die along the Thames
Thus silently! Now every sail is furl'd,
The oar hath dropt from out the rower's hand,
And on thou flow'st in lifeless majesty,
River of a desert lately filled with joy!
O'er all that mighty wilderness of stone
The air is clear and cloudless as at sea
Above the gliding ship. All fires are dead,
And not one single wreath of smoke ascends
Above the stillness of the towers and spires.
How idly hangs that arch magnificent
Across the idle river! Not a speck
Is seen to move along it. There it hangs,
Still as a rainbow in the pathless sky.
   Wil. Methinks such words bespeak a soul at rest,
And willing, in this universal calm,
To abide, whate'er it be, the doom of Fate.
   Frank. I feel as if such solemn images
Of desolation had recall'd my soul
From its own individual wretchedness;
As if one moment I forgot my parent,
And all the friends I love, in the sublime
And overwhelming presence of mortality.

Scene I: THE CITY OF THE PLAGUE.   7

Wil. Now, that your soul feels strong, let us proceed,
With humble hope, towards your mother's house.

Frank. No, friend! here must we part! If e'er again
We meet in this sad world, thou may'st behold
A wretch bow'd down to the earth by misery,
Ghost-like 'mid living men; but rest assur'd,
O gentlest friend! that, though my soul be dead
To all beside, at sight of thee 'twill burn
As with the everlasting fires of joy,
Bursting its bonds of mortal wretchedness.

Wil. We must not—will not part.

Frank.   Now, and for ever.
I walk into yon city as the tomb!
A voice comes to me from its silent towers,
" Mortal, thy days are number'd!" Ere I go,
Kiss me, and promise that my name shall live
Sacred for ever in thy memory.

Wil. We must not—will not part.

Frank.   What said my friend?

Wil. Here, by my father's soul (a fearless man,
Who us'd to say he never lov'd his friends
But in their combats with adversity,)
I swear (and may we never meet in Heaven
If that dread oath be broken) day and night,
Long as thou sojourn'st on thy work of love
Within this plague-struck city, at thy side
To move for ever an attending shadow;
Amid the silence or the shrieks of death,

Serene in unappalled confidence,
That thou wilt walk unharm'd, wilt find the house
Of thy parent, and her holy family
Pass'd over by the angel of the Lord!
For the blessings of the poor have sanctified
The widow's lowly porch—life still is there.

Frank. O friend! most cruel from excess of love!
In all the beauty of thy untam'd spirit
Thou walkest to perdition. Do not I
Look, as I feel, most like thy murderer?
Return unto our ship.

Wil. Frankfort, remember
When the wild cry, " A man is overboard,"
Rung through our decks, till dumb and motionless
Stood the whole crew, fear-stricken by the storm.
Who at that moment leapt into the sea,
And seiz'd the drowning screamer by the hair?
Who was that glorious being? Who the wretch
Then rescued from the waves? I lov'd thee well
Before I hung upon thy saving arm
Above the angry waves. But, from that hour,
I felt my soul call'd on by Providence
To dedicate itself for aye to thee,
And God's will must be done.

Frank. Wilmot, dost think
My mother can be living?

Wil. The soul oft feels
Mysterious presence of realities

Coming we know not whence, yet banishing
With power omnipotent all misgiving fears.
So feel I at this moment—she is living.

Frank. O God forbid ! that I should place belief
In these dim shadowings of futurity.
Here, on this very spot where now we rest,
Upon the morning I last sail'd from England,
My mother put her arms around my neck,
And in a solemn voice, unchok'd by tears,
Said, " Son ! a last farewell !" That solemn voice,
Amid the ocean's roaring solitude,
Oft past across my soul, and I have heard it
Steal in sad music from the sunny calm.
Upon our homeward voyage, when we spake
The ship that told us of the Plague, I knew
That the trumpet's voice would send into our souls
Some dismal tidings ; for I saw her sails
Black in the distance, flinging off with scorn
A shower of radiance from the blessed sun,
As if her crew would not be comforted.

Wil. The weakness of affection, prone to fear !
Be comforted by me—my very dreams
Of late have all been joyous.

Frank. Joyous dreams !
My hours of sleep are now but few indeed,
Yet what have I still dreamt of ? healthful faces,
Round a sweet fire-side, bright with gratitude ?
The soft voice of domestic happiness ?

Laughter disturbing with the stir of joy
The reveries of the spirit?—Oh! my friend!
Far other sounds and sights have fill'd my dreams!
Still noiseless floors, untrod by human feet;
Chairs standing rueful in their emptiness;
An unswept hearth chok'd up by dust and ashes;
Beds with their curtains idly hanging down
Unmov'd by the breath of life; wide open windows
That the fresh air might purify the room
From vapours of the noisome pestilence;
In a dark chamber, ice-cold like a tomb,
A corpse laid out—O God! my mother's corpse
Woefully altered by a dire decay;
While my stunn'd spirit shudder'd at the toll,
The long, slow, dreary, sullen, mortal toll
Of a bell swinging to the hand of death.
But this is idle raving—hope is gone—
And fears and apprehensions, day and night,
Drive where they will my unresisting soul.

Wil. But that it is day-light, I could believe
That yonder, moving by the river side,
Came on a ghost. Did ever eye behold
A thing so death-like in the shape of man?

[*An old man of a miserable and squalid appearance
 comes up, carrying an infant in his arms.*]

Frank. God's blessing on thee! wilt thou rest, old
  man,
Upon this traveller's seat?

Scene I.   THE CITY OF THE PLAGUE.

   Old Man.   God's blessing on thee!
What, dost thou mean to taunt with mockery
An old man tottering to the grave? What pleasure
Can ye young wretches find in scoffing thus
At the white head of hunger'd beggary?
Have ye no fathers? Well it is for them
That their dry hearts are spar'd the bitterness
Of seeing, in the broad and open day,
Their reckless children sporting with old age.
   Frank. Father, judge kindly of us.
   Old Man.   Let me go
Untroubled on my way. Do you pity me?
Then give me alms: this thing upon my arm
Is teasing me for food: I have it not—
Give me your alms.
   Frank.   See! here is bread, old man!
I ask your blessing—come you from the city,
And none to guide your steps along the brink
Of this great river?
   Old Man.   Yea! they all are dead
Who once did walk with me most lovingly,
Slowlier than these slow steps. This piece of wood,
This staff, is all I have to lean on now,
And this poor baby, whom its nurse would give
For a short pastime to his grandsire's arms,
No other nurse hath now, but wither'd age—
Sour, sullen, hopeless, God-forsaken age.
   Frank. Is the Plague raging?

Old Man. Aye, and long will rage.
The judgments of the prophets of old time
Are now fulfilling. Young men turn and flee
From the devoted city. Would ye hear
What now is passing in yon monster's heart?

Frank. We listen to thy voice.

Old Man. Three months ago
Within my soul I heard a mighty sound
As of a raging river, day and night
Triumphing through the city: 'twas the voice
Of London sleepless in magnificence.
This morn I stood and listen'd. " Art thou dead,
Queen of the world!" I ask'd my awe-struck heart,
And not one breath of life amid the silence
Disturb'd the empire of mortality.
Death's icy hand hath frozen, with a touch,
The fountain of the river that made glad
The City of the Isle!

Frank. We hear thy voice.

Old Man. Sin brought the judgment: it was terrible.
Go read your Bible, young men; hark to him
Who, in a vision, saw the Lion rage
Amid the towers of Judah, while the people
Fell on their faces, and the hearts of kings
Perish'd, and prophets wonder'd in their fear.
Then came the dry wind from the wilderness,
Towards the hill of Sion, not to fan

Or cleanse, but, whirlwind-like, to sweep away
The tents of princes and the men of war.
   Frank. Wilmot! methinks most like an ancient prophet,
With those white locks and wild unearthly eyes,
He comes forth from the desolated city,
A man who cannot die. O may I ask,
Most reverend father, if——
   Old Man.   Hush! hush! lie still!—
Didst hear this infant cry? So small a sound
Ought not to startle thus a wretch who comes
From a three-months' sojourn in a sepulchre.
Here! infant, eat this bread, and hold thy peace.
Young men, disturb me not with foolish questions;
Your faces are towards the city: Will ye dare
The monster in his den? Then go and die!
Two little drops amid a shower of rain,
Swallowed up in a moment by the heedless earth.
   Frank. I fain would ask one question; for, old man,
My parent lived in London, and I go
To seek her in that city of the tombs.
   Old Man. Think of her with the dead! A ship at sea
(Methinks I speak unto a mariner)
Goes to the bottom. Would you hope to find
Your friend alone, of all the fated crew,
Alive on a plank next day amid the waves?
Think of her with the dead! and praise the Lord!
   Wilmot. Let us begone, the day is wearing fast.

Old Man. Know ye what you will meet with in the
    city?
Together will ye walk, through long, long streets,
All standing silent as a midnight church.
You will hear nothing but the brown red grass
Rustling beneath your feet; the very beating
Of your own hearts will awe you; the small voice
Of that vain bauble, idly counting time,
Will speak a solemn language in the desert.
Look up to heaven, and there the sultry clouds,
Still threatening thunder, lower with grim delight,
As if the Spirit of the plague dwelt there,
Darkening the city with the shadows of death.
Know ye that hideous hubbub? Hark, far off
A tumult like an echo! on it comes,
Weeping and wailing, shrieks and groaning prayer;
And louder than all outrageous blasphemy.
The passing storm hath left the silent streets.
But are these houses near you tenantless?
Over your heads from a window, suddenly
A ghastly face is thrust, and yells of death
With voice not human. Who is he that flies,
As if a demon dogg'd him on his path?
With ragged hair, white face, and bloodshot eyes,
Raving, he rushes past you; till he falls,
As if struck by lightning, down upon the stones,
Or, in blind madness, dash'd against the wall,
Sinks backward into stillness. Stand aloof,

And let the Pest's triumphal chariot
Have open way advancing to the tomb.
See how he mocks the pomp and pageantry
Of earthly kings! A miserable cart,
Heap'd up with human bodies; dragg'd along
By pale steeds, skeleton-anatomies!
And onwards urged by a wan meagre wretch,
Doom'd never to return from the foul pit,
Whither, with oaths, he drives his load of horror.
Would you look in? Grey hairs and golden tresses,
Wan shrivell'd cheeks that have not smil'd for years;
And many a rosy visage smiling still;
Bodies in the noisome weeds of beggary wrapt,
With age decrepit, and wasted to the bone;
And youthful frames, august and beautiful,
In spite of mortal pangs,—there lie they all
Embrac'd in ghastliness! But look not long,
For haply, 'mid the faces glimmering there,
The well-known cheek of some beloved friend
Will meet thy gaze, or some small snow-white hand,
Bright with the ring that holds her lover's hair.
Let me sit down beside you. I am faint
Talking of horrors that I look'd upon
At last without a shudder.

   Frank.   Give me the child.

   Old Man. Let the wretch rest. 'Twas but a passing
      pang,
And I feel strong again. Dost smile, poor babe?

Yes! Thou art glad to see the full-orb'd eye,
The placid cheek, and sparkling countenance
Of ruddy health once more; and thou wouldst go
With them thy young heart thinks so beautiful,
Nor ever look behind at the old man
Who brought thee from the grave! Sweet thoughtless
    wretch,
I cling to thee with a more desperate love
Because of thy ingratitude.

 Frank.   Old man,
Is thy blood in his veins?

 Old Man.   All dead—all dead!
Round the baptismal font with awe we knelt,
My four sweet daughters and their loving husbands.
I held my last-born grandchild in my arms,
But as the hallow'd water touch'd her face,
Even then she sicken'd, and a mortal paleness
Froze every parent's cheek. "The Plague is here,"
The priest exclaim'd; and like so many ghosts,
We parted in the church-yard. O my God!
I know that Thou in wrath art merciful,
For Thou hast spar'd this babe for my old age!
But all who knelt round that baptismal font
Last Sabbath morning—one short week ago—
Are dead and buried—save one little child,
And a grey-headed man of fourscore years.

 Frank. I dare not comfort thee.

 Old Man.   Why not, sweet youth!

Thy very voice is comfort—my dim eyes
Look on thee like a vision of delight
Coming back in beauty from th' abyss of years.
Let me hear thy voice once more!

 Frank.   Father! that book
With whose worn leaves the careless infant plays
Must be the Bible. Therein thy dim eyes
Will meet a cheering light, and silent words
Of mercy breath'd from heaven, will be exhal'd
From the blest page into thy wither'd heart.
The grace of God go with thee.

 Old Man.   Gentle youth!
Thy voice reminds me of a boy who died
Thirty long years ago. Thou wilt pass on,
And we must meet no more; yet could I think
Thou wert my son returning from the grave,
Or from some far-off land where he had gone
And left us to our tears.

 Frank.   They are not lost
Who leave their parents for the calm of heaven.
Forgive a young man speaking thus to age,
'Tis done in love and reverence.

 Old Man.   'Tis the Bible!
I know and feel it is a blessed book,
And I remember how it stopp'd my tears
In days of former sorrows, like some herb
Of sovereign virtue to a wound applied.
But thou wilt pity me, when I confess

That ofttimes more than mortal agony
Shoots through my heart, when the most holy words
Of Jesus shine before me. There I see
Miracles of mercy and of saving love:
The widow sings for joy,—deliverance
Comes to the madman howling in his chains,—
And life stirs in the tomb. I shut the book,
And wonder where I am; for all around me
Looks as if God had left this woeful earth
To ruin and despair, while his own word
Doth seem delusion, or with fearful doubts
My soul disturbs in sore perplexity.
To the Hebrew prophecies my spirit turns,
And feeds on wailing lamentations,
And dim forebodings of Almighty wrath.
Yea! often do I see this very Plague
By these wild seers foretold, and all their songs
So doleful speak unto my ringing ear
Of this dread visitation. Idle dreams
Of my old crazed brain! But aye they haunt me,
And each plain phrase is cloth'd with mystic meaning
In spite of reason; sad bewildering!
When still the soul keeps fighting with its fetters,
Yet hugs them self-impos'd.

   Frank.   Such dreams will vanish
When the sweet rural air, or breeze from the sea
Sings round thee. Art thou going to a home
Where wife or child expect thee?

Old Man.   Hush, sweet babe.
There is a dwelling on the lone sea-shore
Where I will carry thee.—An Angel's voice
Told me to leave the city. You will see her,
The Angel of the poor! Through every street
The radiant Creature walks......
   Wil. to Frank.   Though dark his brain,
It has, thou seest, a heavenly visitor,
That comfort brings when reason's self is gone.
   Old Man. 'Tis no delusion. When you see her face,
Her pale face smiling on you suddenly,
Pale almost as the raiment that she wears,
And hear her voice, all one low mournful tone,
Charming away despair, then will ye say
" The Angel this of whom the old man spake ;"
Yet something lying far within her eyes
Will tell that she is mortal.—Fare ye well!
But list! sweet youths! where'er ye go, beware
Of those dread dwellings all round Aldgate-church,
For to me it seemeth that most dismal pile
Is the black Palace of the Plague, and none
May pass it by and live. God bless you both.
                         [*The Old Man passes on.*]
   Frank. His words have sent a curse into my heart.
The miserable spoke of misery
Even with his parting farewell. Aldgate-church!
   Wil. He passeth like a shadow from the city!
A solemn traveller to the world of spirits.

Methought his hollow and unearthly voice
Came from the desolation of his soul
Like the wind at midnight moaning past our ship,
A ghastly sound once heard and never more.
—Frankfort speak to me.

Frank. All round Aldgate-church!
Said he not so? Close to that church-yard wall
My mother's dwelling stands; her bed-room window
Looks o'er the grave-stones and the marble tombs.—
All hope is dead within me.

Wil. Shall I go
And ask the old man if he knows your mother,
Perhaps......

Frank. Oh! ask him not, an hour will bring us
In presence of the house where I was born.
I wish he had staid with us yet a while,
For his voice held me in captivity,
Wild voice and haggard cheek. He heeded not
Me or my sorrow—in his misery
Both blind and deaf, without the help of age.
Methinks I see the cold wet tombstone lying
Upon my father's grave—another name,
" Mary his wife," is graven......

Wil. All have not perish'd.

Frank. What, hoping still! Come, let us onwards walk
With heads uncover'd, and with prostrate souls,
Unto the humbled city of despair.
Amid the roar of ocean-solitude

God hath been with us, and his saving hand
Will be our anchor in this dreadful calm,
This waveless silence of the sea of death.

SCENE II.

A great square in the city.—A multitude of miserable men and women crowding round a person of a wild and savage appearance, dressed in a fantastical garb, with an hour-glass in his hand.

Astrologer. The sun is going down, and when he sets,
You know my accursed gift of prophecy
Departeth from me, and I then become
Blind as my wretched brethren. Then the Plague
Riots in darkness 'mid his unknown victims,
Nor can I read the names within his roll
Now register'd in characters of blood.
Come to me all ye wearied who would rest,
Who would exchange the fever's burning pillow
For the refreshing coolness of the grave!
Come hither all ye orphans of a day,
And I will tell you when your heads shall rest
Upon your parents' bosoms. Yearn ye not
To clasp their shroudless bodies, and to lie
In the dark pit by love made beautiful!
Where are ye veiled widows? in the tomb
The marriage-lamp doth burn unquenchably.
Dry up your tears, fair virgins! to the grave
Betrothed in your pure simplicity!

Still is one countenance beautiful in death,
And it will lean to-night upon a breast
White with the snows of perfect innocence.
—I call upon the wicked! let him shew
His face among the crowd, and I will tell him
His dreams of horror and his works of sin.

   [*A man of a fierce and ferocious aspect advances from the crowd.*]

  Stranger. I ask thee not, thou juggling driveller,
Whether the Plague hath fix'd his eyes on me,
Determin'd to destroy. Let them who fear
Death and his pit, with pale beseeching hands
Buy with their monies the awards of fate,
And die in poverty. Thou speak'st of guilt,
And know'st forsooth each secret deed of sin
Done in the dark hour. Tell me, driveller!
Where I, who lay no claim to honesty,
Came by this gold. I'll give thee half of it
If thou speak'st truly. Was there robbery?

  Astrologer. Flee murderer! from my sight! I touch thy gold!
'Twould stain my fingers! See the blood-gouts on it.
Hither thou com'st in savage hardihood,
Yet with a beating heart. I saw thee murder him;
What were his silver hairs, his tremulous voice,
His old blind eyes to thee!—Ha! shrinking off,
Aw'd by a driveller! Seize the murderer!

You will find the bloody knife——
    [*The man rushes off, and all make way for him.*]
    Astrologer.   Mine eyes at once
Did read the murderer's soul.
    Voice from the crowd.   Guilt nor disease
Are hidden from his ken—he knows them all.
        [*Two women advance eagerly from the crowd.*]
    1st *Woman.* Listen to me before that woman speaks.
I went this morning to my lover's house,
Mine own betrothed husband, who had come
From sea two days ago.   The house was empty;
As the cold grave that longeth for its coffin
'Twas damp and empty; and I shriek'd in vain
On him who would not hear.   Tell me his fate,
Say that he lives, or say that he is dead—
But tell me,—tell me, lest I curse my God,
Some tidings of him; should'st thou see him lying
Even in yon dreadful pit. Do you hear? speak, speak!
O God!—no words can be so terrible
As that mute face whose blackness murders hope,
And freezes my sick soul.   Heaven's curse light on thee,
For that dumb mockery of a broken heart!
    Astrologer. I see him not, some cloud envelopes him!
    Woman. He hath left the city then, and gone on ship-
        board?
    Astrologer. I see him not, some cloud envelopes him!
    Woman. What! hast thou not a wond'rous glass that
        shews

Things past, or yet to come? give me one look,
That I may see his face so beautiful,
Where'er it be; or in that ghastly pit,
Or smiling 'mid his comrades on the deck,
While favouring breezes waft his blessed ship
Far from the Plague, to regions of delight
Where he may live for ever.

Astrologer. Is your lover
A tall thin youth, with thickly-clustering locks,
Sable and glossy as the raven's wing?

Woman. Yes! he is tall—I think that he is tall,
His hair it is dark-brown—yes, almost black—
Many call it black—you see him? Does he live?

Astrologer. That pit containeth many beautiful:
But thy sailor in his warlike garb doth lie
Distinguish'd o'er the multitude of dead!
And all the crowd, when the sad cart was emptied,
Did weep and sob for that young mariner;
Such corpse, they thought, should have been buried
Deep in the ocean's heart, and a proud peal
Of thunder roll'd above his sinking coffin.

Woman, (distractedly.) Must I believe him? off, off
  to the pit!
One look into that ghastliness,—one plunge:
None ever lov'd me but my gentle sailor,
And his sweet lips are cold—I will leap down.

[*She rushes madly away.*]

Voice from the crowd. Aye, she intends to look before
    she leaps;
Well—life is life—I would not part with it
For all the girls in Christendom. Forsooth!
  2d Woman. Say! will my child recover from the
    Plague?
  Astrologer. Child! foolish woman! now thou hast no
    child.
Hast thou not been from home these two long hours,
Here listening unto that which touch'd thee not,
And left'st thou not thy little dying child,
Sitting by the fire, upon a madman's knee?
Go home! and ask thy husband for thy child!
The fire was burning fierce and wrathfully,
Its father knew not that the thing he held
Upon his knee had life—and when it shriek'd,
Amid the flames, he sat and look'd at it,
With fixed eyeballs, and a stony heart.
Unnatural mother! worse than idiotcy
To leave a baby in a madman's lap,
And yet no fetters from infanticide
To save his murderous hands.
  Woman, (rushing away.)   O God! O God!
  Astrologer. Come forward thou with that most ghost-
    like face,
Fit for a winding-sheet! and if those lips
So blue and quivering still can utter sounds,
What would'st thou say? The motions of thine eyes

Betoken some wild wish within thy heart.
  [*A man comes forward, and lays down money be-
  fore the Astrologer.*]

Man. I trust my hour is near. I am alone
In this dark world, and I desire to die.

Astrologer. Thou shalt be kept alive by misery.
A tree doth live, long after rottenness
Hath eat away its heart: the sap of life
Moves through its wither'd rind, and it lives on;
'Mid the green woods a rueful spectacle
Of mockery and decay.

Man.   I feel 'tis so.
Thus have I been since first the Plague burst out,
A term methinks of many hundred years!
As if this world were hell, and I condemn'd
To walk through woe to all eternity.
I will do suicide.

Astrologer.   Thou can'st not fool!
Thou lovest life with all its agonies:
Buy poison, and 'twill lie for years untouch'd
Beneath thy pillow, when thy midnight horrors
Are at their worst. Coward! thou can'st not die!

Man. He sees my soul; a blast as if from hell
Drives me back from the grave—I dare not die.
  [*He disappears among the crowd, and a young and
  beautiful lady approaches the Astrologer.*]

Lady. O man of fate! my lovely babes are dead!
My sweet twin-babes! and at the very hour

Thy voice predicted, did my infants die.
My husband saw them both die in my arms,
And never shed a tear. Yet did he love them
Even as the wretch who bore them in her womb.
He will not speak to me, but ever sits
In horrid silence, with his glazed eyes
Full on my face, as if he lov'd me not—
O God! as if he hated me! I lean
My head upon his knees and say my prayers,
But no kind word, or look, or touch is mine.
Then will he rise and pace through all the rooms,
Like to a troubled ghost, or pale-fac'd man
Walking in his sleep. O tell me! hath the Plague
E'er these wild symptoms? Must my husband perish
Without the sense of his immortal soul?
Or,—bless me for ever with the heavenly words,—
Say he will yet recover, and behold
His loving wife with answering looks of love.

Astrologer. Where are the gold, the diamonds and the
    pearls,
That erewhile, in thy days of vanity,
Did sparkle, star-like, through the hanging clouds
That shaded thy bright neck, that raven hair?
Give them to me; for many are the poor,
Nor shalt thou, Lady! ever need again
This mortal being's frivolous ornaments.
Give me the gold you promis'd; holiest alms
Add not a moment to our number'd days,

But the death of open-handed charity
Is on a bed of down. Hast thou the gold?

   Lady. All that I have is here. My husband gave me
This simple necklace on my marriage-day.
Take it! Here is a picture set in gold.
The picture I may keep. O! that his face
Were smiling so serenely beautiful,
So like an angel's now!—O sacred ring!
Which I did hope to wear within the tomb,
I give thee to the poor. So may their prayers
Save him from death for whose delightful sake
With bliss I wore it, and with hope resign.
Here, take them all, thou steward of the poor;
Stern as thou art, thou art a holy man!
I do believe thou art a holy man.

   Astrologer. Lady, thou need'st this wedding-ring no more!
Death with his lean and bony hand hath loosen'd
The bauble from thy finger, and even now
Thy husband is a corpse. O! might I say
Thy beauty were immortal! But a ghost,
In all the loveliness on earth it wore,
Walks through the moonlight of the cemetery,
And I know the shadow of the mortal creature
Now weeping at my side.

Scene II. THE CITY OF THE PLAGUE.

Enter FRANKFORT *and* WILMOT *close to the Astrologer.*

 Frank.   Amelia!
 Lady. Ah me! whose soft kind voice is that I hear?
 Frank. Frankfort! the playmate of thy infancy,
The brother of thy womanhood, the friend
Of thy dear husband, and the godfather
Of thy sweet twins, heaven shield their innocence!
 Lady. My babes are with their Saviour, and my husband
Has gone with them to heaven. Lead, lead me hence!
For the seer's stern and scowling countenance
Is more than I can bear.
 Frank.   O grief! to think
That one so dear to heaven, by Christ belov'd
For a still life of perfect sinlessness,
Should, in such sad delusion, court the ban
Of this most savage liar, sporting thus
With the broken spirit of humanity.
 Astrologer. Welcome to London, storm-beat mariners!
The city is in masquerade to-day,
And, in good truth, the Plague doth celebrate
A daily festival, with many a dance
Fantastic, and unusual melody,
That may not suit your ears accustom'd long
To the glad sea-breeze, and the rousing airs
Of martial music on your armed decks.

Frank. to Wil. Is this some wild enthusiast whom the times
Have sent unto the light, deluding others
By his own strong delusions, or some fiend
Thirsting for gold even in the very grave?
   Wil. With what a cruel face he looks at us!
   Frank. If an impostor in the shadow of death
Endangering thus thy soul, vile wretch! come down
From thy tribunal built upon the fears
Of agony, lest in thy seat of guile
The Pest may smite thee! Lean on me, Amelia!
   Astrologer. Scoff not at God's own delegate, Harry Frankfort!
What though the burning fever of the west
Hath spar'd thy bronzed face and stately form,
A mightier Power is here; and he may smile,
Ere the sun go down, upon thy bloated corpse.
Not thus the maiden whom her sailor loves
Despis'd me and my prophecies. Magdalene
In snow-white raiment, like a maid that walk'd
At the funeral of a maiden, she stood there,
Even on the very stones beneath your feet,
And ask'd of me her doom; but on this earth
Thy Magdalene's beauty must be seen no more.
   Frank. to Wil. The maid of whom he speaks lives far remote.
In her father's cottage, near a silent lake
Among the hills of Westmoreland, she breathes,

Scene II.   THE CITY OF THE PLAGUE.

Happy and well, her own sweet mountain air.
Methinks I know his face.   That harden'd eye
Gleams through the dimness of my memory,
I know not when nor where.   Amelia, come
And I will lead thee home.   I hear the crowd
Saying that thy husband is alive: may heaven
For many a year preserve you to each other.
Say, is my mother living?

  Lady.   God forgive me,
As I hope for my friend's forgiveness!
I know not if she lives; for, oh! this Plague
Hath spread an universal selfishness,
And each house in its own calamity
Stands single, shut from human fellowship
By sullen misery and heart-withering fear.

  Voice from the crowd. Look at the sorcerer! how his
    countenance
Is fallen!—'tis distorted horribly!
A shadow comes across it, like a squall
Dark'ning the sea.

  Another voice. Even thus I saw a man
This very morning stricken by the Plague,
And in three hours he was a ghost.   Disperse
All ye who prize your lives! soon will the air
Be foul with his dead body.   Let us away!
           [*The crowd disperse.*]

 Astrologer. God's hand is on me.   In my cruel guilt
I perish.   Frankfort, I have never seen

Magdalene, the maid thou lovest. Look at me;
Dost not remember Francis Bannerman
On board the Thunderer?

 Frank.   Pardon to thy soul!
Thou mad abuser of the gifts of heaven.

 Astrologer. Oh! I am sick to death; my soul hath
  sunk
At once into despair.

 Wil.   What dreadful groans!—
O fatal is the blast of misery,
When it hath forc'd its way into the soul
Of harden'd cruelty! As when a storm
Hath burst the gates of a thick-ribbed hold,
And all its gloomy dungeons, in one moment,
Are roaring like a hundred cataracts.

 Astrologer. I have shed blood. Roll, roll ye moun-
  tain waves,
Above that merciless ghost that walks the sea
After our ship for ever! Shut thine eyes,
Those glaring, bloodshot, those avenging eyes,
And I will bear to feel thy skeleton-arms
Twin'd round my heart, so that those eyes be shut!
A ghost's wild eyes, that nothing can behold
But the frighten'd aspect of its murderer!
Unconscious they of ocean, air, and Heaven,
But fix'd eternally, like hideous stars,
On a shrieking soul whom guilt hath doom'd to Hell!

 Frank. to Wil. The mutineer is raving of his crime.

Astrologer. Ha! ha! 'tis set within the ebb of flood
Fifty feet high; and the iron'd criminal
With a frantic face stands dumb upon the scaffold.
The priest is singing psalms!—Curst be the eyes
That see such idle shew—'tis all gone by!
I fear not Hell, if that eternal Shape
Meet me not there! Pray, pray not for me Frankfort,
For I am deliver'd over to despair,
And holy words are nought but mockery
To him who knows that he must dwell for ever
In regions darken'd by the wrath of God.

Lady. Let us leave this horrid scene!

Astrologer. O might I hear
That sweet voice breathing of forgiveness!
Hush! hush! a voice once breath'd upon this earth
That would have pleaded not in vain to Heaven,
Even for a fiend like me. Thou art in Heaven,
And knowest all thy husband's wickedness;
So hide thy pitying eyes, and let me sink
Without thy intercession to the depths
Of unimagin'd woe!——O Christ! I die.

Frank. Most miserable end! an evil man
Prostrating by a savage eloquence
The spirits of the wretched—so that he
Might riot on the bare necessities
Of man's expiring nature—on the spoil
Of the unburied dead! Most atheist-like!
I know not how I can implore the grace
Of God unto thy soul!

Astrologer.   Eternal doom!
The realms of Hell are gleaming fiery bright.
What ghastly faces!—Christ, have mercy on me!

Lady. Wilt thou not lead me away, for I am blind!
O Frankfort come with me—the Plague hath struck
My husband into madness—and I fear him!
O God! I fear the man whom I do love!

Frank. All—all are wretched—guilty—dead or dying;
And all the wild and direful images
That crowd, and wail, and blacken round my soul
Have reconcil'd me to the misery
Sent from my mother's grave.   An hour of respite
Is granted me while I conduct thee home:
Then will I seek that grave, and 'mid the tumult
Of this perturbed city sit and listen
To a voice that in my noiseless memory
Sings like an angel.

Lady.   She is yet alive!

Frank. Thy voice is like the voice of Hope—Sweet
     friend,
Be cheer'd, nor tremble so—for God is with us.

SCENE III.

A Church-yard.—Two Females in mourning dresses sitting on a Tombstone.

1*st Lady.* The door of the Cathedral is left open.
Perhaps some one within is at the altar
Offering up thanks, or supplicating heaven
To save a husband dying of the Plague.

If so, I join a widow's prayer to hers,
Sitting on my husband's grave.

   2d Lady.   One moment hush!
Methought I heard a footstep in the church
As of one walking softly up the chancel.
List—list! I am not dreaming of a strain
Of heav'nly music? 'Tis a hymn of praise.

          [*A voice is heard singing in the Cathedral.*]

   1st Lady. A voice so heavenly sweet I once did hear
Singing at night close to my bed, when I
Was beyond hope recovering from the Plague.
That voice hymn'd in my sleep and was a dream
Framed by my soul returning unto life,
A strain that murmur'd from another world.
But this is earthly music: she must have
An angel's face who through the echoing aisle
So like an angel sings.

   2d Lady.   I know that voice!
Last Sabbath evening, sitting on this stone,
And thinking who it was that lay below it,
I heard that very music faint and far,
Deaden'd almost into silence by the weight
Of those thick walls. I listen'd with my heart
That I might hear the dirge-like air again.
But it did rise no more, and I believ'd
'Twas some sweet fancy of my sorrowful soul,
Or wandering breath of evening through the pillars
Of the Cathedral sighing wildly by.

1st Lady. And sawest thou no one?

2d Lady.   Yes; I gently stole
Into the solemn twilight of the church,
And looking towards the altar, there I saw
A white-rob'd Being on her knees. At first
I felt such awe as I had seen a spirit,
When, rising from the attitude of prayer
The vision softly glided down the steps,
And then her eyes met mine. But such sweet eyes,
So fill'd with human sadness, yet so bright
Even through their tears with a celestial joy
Ne'er shone before on earth. Even such methought
The Virgin-Mother's holy countenance,
When, turning from her Son upon the cross,
A gleam of heavenly comfort cheer'd the darkness
Of her disconsolate soul! At once I knew
That I was looking on the Maid divine
Whom the sad city bless'd—whose form arises
Beside the bed of death by all deserted,
And to the dim eyes of the dying man
Appears an angel sent from pitying heaven
To bid him part in peace. I could have dropt
Down on my knees and worshipp'd her, but silent
As a gleam of light the creature glided by me,
And e'er my soul recover'd she was gone.

1st Lady. How weak and low does virtue such as hers
Make us poor beings feel.

2d Lady.   Yet she is one

Of frail and erring mortals, and she knew not
In other days, to what a lofty pitch
Her gentle soul could soar. For I have heard
She was an only child, and in the light
Of her fond parents' love was fostered,
Like a flower that blooms best shelter'd in the house,
And only plac'd beneath the open air
In hours of sunshine.

  1st Lady.   Could we now behold
The glorious Being?

  2d Lady.   No: this hour is sacred;
We must not interrupt her. The dew falls
Heavy and chill, and thou art scarce recover'd
From that long sickness.—Let me kiss thee thus,
Thou cold wet stone,—thou loveliest, saddest name,
Ever engraven on a monument.

 [*The scene changes to the interior of the Cathedral.* MAG-
  DALENE *discovered on her knees at the altar.*]

 Magdalene. Father of mercies! may I lift mine eyes
From the holy ground that I have wet with tears,
Unto the silence of the moonlight heavens
That shine above me with a smile of love,
Forgiveness, and compassion. There Thou art!
Enthron'd in glory and omnipotence!
Yet from thy dwelling 'mid the eternal stars,
Encircled by the hymning seraphim,
Thou dost look down upon our mortal earth,
And seest this weeping creature on her knees,

And hear'st the beatings of her lonely heart.
If, in my days of sinless infancy,
My innocence found favour in thy sight;
If in my youth,—and yet I am but young,—
I strove to walk according to thy will,
And reverenc'd my Bible, and did weep,
Thinking of him who died upon the cross;
If, in their old age, I did strive to make
My parents happy, and receiv'd at last
Their benediction on the bed of death—
Oh! let me walk the waves of this wild world
Through faith unsinking;—stretch thy saving hand
To a lone castaway upon the sea,
Who hopes no resting-place except in heaven.
And oh! this holy calm,—this peace profound,—
That sky so glorious in infinitude,—
That countless host of softly-burning stars,
And all that floating universe of light,
Lift up my spirit far above the grave,
And tell me that my pray'rs are heard in Heaven
I feel th' Omnipotent is Merciful!

[*A voice exclaims from an unseen person,*]
O were my name remember'd in thy pray'rs!

   Magd. (*rising from her knees.*) Did some one speak?

   Voice.   A sinful wretch implores
That thou wilt stand between him and the wrath
Of an offended God.

   Magd.   Come to the altar.

[*A man advances from behind a pillar, and kneels down at the altar.*]

Stranger. I fear I cannot pray. My wicked heart,
Long unaccustom'd to these bended knees,
Feels not the worship that my limbs would offer;
—My lot is cast in hell.

Magd.   Repentance finds
The blackest gulf in the wild soul of sin,
And calms the tumult there, even as our Lord
With holy hand did hush the howling sea.

Stranger. Lady! I am too near thy blessed side;
The breath of such a saint ought not to fall
Into the hard heart of a murderer.

Magd. Hast thou come here to murder me?

Stranger.   Behold
This cruel knife.

Magd.   The will of God be done!

Stranger. Rather than hurt one of those loveliest hairs
That braided round thy pale, thy fearless brow,
Do make thee seem an Angel or a Spirit
At night come down from heaven, would I for ever
Live in the dark corruption of the grave.

Magd. My heart is beating—but I fear thee not—
Thou wilt not murder me?

Stranger.   What need'st thou fear?
Kneeling in those white robes, so like a Spirit,
With face too beautiful for tears to stain,
Eyes meekly raised to heaven, and snow-white hands

Devoutly folded o'er a breast that moves
In silent adoration——what hast thou
To fear from man or fiend? O rise not up!
So Angel-like thou seem'st upon thy knees,
Even I can hope, while thou art at thy prayers.

Magd. If thou cam'st hither to unload thy soul,
Kneel down.

Stranger.　　Sweet one! I came to murder thee.
With silent foot I traced thee to this church,
And there, beyond that pillar, took my stand,
That I might rush upon thee at the altar
And kill thee at thy prayers. I grasp'd the knife—
When suddenly thy melancholy voice
Began that low wild hymn!—I could not move;
The holy music made thee seem immortal!
And when I dared to look towards thy face,
The moonlight fell upon it, and I saw
A smile of such majestic innocence
That long-lost pity to my soul return'd,
And I knelt down and wept.

Magd.　　　　　　What made thee think
Of killing one who never injured thee?

Stranger. Th' accursed love of gold.

Magd.　　　　　　　　Hath Poverty
Blinded thy soul, and driven thee forth a prey
To Sin who loves the gaunt and hollow cheeks
Of miserable men? Perhaps a cell
Holds thy sick wife——

Scene III.   THE CITY OF THE PLAGUE.

Stranger.   No! I have sold my soul
Unto the Evil One, nor even can'st Thou,
With all the music of that heavenly voice,
Charm the stern ear of hell.
Magd.   Alas, poor wretch!
What shakes thee so?
Stranger.   Mid all the ghastly shrieking,
Black sullen dumbness, and wild-staring frenzy,
Pain madly leaping out of life, or fetter'd
By burning irons to its house of clay,
Where think you Satan drove me? To the haunts
Of riot, lust, and reckless blasphemy.
In spite of that eternal passing-bell,
And all the ghosts that hourly flock'd in troops
Unto the satiated grave, insane
With drunken guilt, I mock'd my Saviour's name
With hideous mummery, and the holy book
In scornful fury trampled, rent, and burn'd.
Oh! ours were dreadful orgies!—At still midnight
We sallied out, in mimic grave-clothes clad,
Aping the dead, and in some church-yard danc'd
A dance that ofttimes had a mortal close.
Then would we lay a living Body out,
As it had been a corpse, and bear it slowly,
With what at distance seem'd a holy dirge,
Through silent streets and squares unto its rest.
One quaintly apparell'd like a surplic'd priest
Led the procession, joining in the song;—

A jestful song, most brutal and obscene,
Shameful to man, his Saviour, and his God.
Or in a hearse we sat, which one did drive
In masquerade-habiliments of death;
And in that ghastly chariot whirl'd along,
With oaths, and songs, and shouts, and peals of laughter,
Till sometimes that most devilish merriment
Chill'd our own souls with horror, and we stared
Upon each other all at once struck dumb.

Magd. Madness! 'twas madness all.

Stranger. Oh! that it were!
But, lady! were we mad when we partook
Of what we call'd a sacrament?

Magd. Hush! hush!—

Stranger. Yes—I will utter it—we brake the bread,
And wine pour'd out, and jesting ate and drank
Perdition to our souls.

Magd. And women too,
Did they blaspheme their Saviour?

Stranger. Aye! there sat
Round that unhallow'd table beautiful Creatures,
Who seem'd to feel a fiend-like happiness
In tempting us wild wretches to blaspheme.
Sweet voices had they, though of broken tones;
Their faces fair, though waxing suddenly
Whiter than ashes; smiles were in their eyes,
Though often in their mirth they upwards look'd,
And wept; nor, when they tore distractedly

The garments from their bosoms, could our souls
Sustain the beauty heaving in our sight
With grief, remorse, despair, and agony.
We knew that we were lost, yet would we pluck
The flowers that bloom'd upon the crater's edge,
Nor fear'd the yawning gulf.

Magd. Why art thou here?

Stranger. Riot hath made us miserably poor,
And gold we needs must have. I heard a whisper
Tempting me to murder, and thy very name
Distinctly syllabled. In vain I strove
Against the Tempter—bent was I on blood!
But here I stand in hopeless penitence,
Nor even implore thy prayers—my doom is seal'd.

[*He flings himself down before the altar.*]

Magd. Poor wretch! I leave thee to the grace of
God.—
Ah me! how calmly and serenely smile
Those pictured saints upon the holy wall,
Tinged by that sudden moonlight! That meek face
How like my mother's! So she wore her veil;
Even so her braided hair!—Ye blessed spirits,
Look down upon your daughter in her trouble,
For I am sick at heart. The moonlight dies—
I feel afraid of darkness. Wretched man,
Hast thou found comfort? Groans his sole reply.—
I must away to that sad Funeral.

SCENE IV.

The street.—A long table covered with glasses.—A party of young men and women carousing.

Young Man. I rise to give, most noble President,
The memory of a man well known to all,
Who by keen jest, and merry anecdote,
Sharp repartee, and humorous remark
Most biting in its solemn gravity,
Much cheer'd our out-door table, and dispell'd
The fogs which this rude visitor the Plague
Oft breathed across the brightest intellect.
But two days past, our ready laughter chaced
His various stories; and it cannot be
That we have in our gamesome revelries
Forgotten Harry Wentworth. His chair stands
Empty at your right hand—as if expecting
That jovial wassailer—but he is gone
Into cold narrow quarters. Well, I deem
The grave did never silence with its dust
A tongue more eloquent; but since 'tis so,
And store of boon companions yet survive,
There is no reason to be sorrowful;
Therefore let us drink unto his memory
With acclamation, and a merry peal
Such as in life he loved.

Master of Revels. 'Tis the first death
Hath been amongst us, therefore let us drink
His memory in silence.

Young Man.   Be it so.
  [*They all rise, and drink their glasses in silence.*]
 Master of Revels. Sweet Mary Gray! Thou hast a
  silver voice,
And wildly to thy native melodies
Can tune it's flute-like breath—sing us a song,
And let it be, even 'mid our merriment,
Most sad, most slow, that when its music dies,
We may address ourselves to revelry,
More passionate from the calm, as men leap up
To this world's business from some heavenly dream.

MARY GRAY'S SONG.

I walk'd by mysel' owre the sweet braes o' Yarrow,
 When the earth wi' the gowans o' July was drest;
But the sang o' the bonny burn sounded like sorrow,
 Round ilka house cauld as a last simmer's nest.

I look'd thro' the lift o' the blue smiling morning,
 But never ae wee cloud o' mist could I see
On its way up to heaven the cottage adorning,
 Hanging white owre the green o' it's sheltering tree.

By the outside I ken'd that the in was forsaken,
 That nae tread o' footsteps was heard on the floor;
—O loud craw'd the cock whare was nane to awaken,
 And the wild-raven croak'd on the seat by the door!

Sic silence—sic lonesomeness, oh! were bewildering!
 I heard nae lass singing when herding her sheep;

I met nae bright garlands o' wee rosy children
　　Dancing on to the school-house just wakened frae sleep.

I past by the school-house—when strangers were coming,
　　Whose windows with glad faces seem'd all alive;
Ae moment I hearken'd, but heard nae sweet humming,
　　For a night o' dark vapour can silence the Hive.

I past by the pool whare the lasses at daw'ing
　　Used to bleach their white garments wi' daffin and din;
But the foam in the silence o' nature was fa'ing,
　　And nae laughing rose loud thro' the roar o' the linn.

I gaed into a small town—when sick o' my roaming—
　　Whare ance play'd the viol, the tabor and flute;
'Twas the hour lov'd by Labour, the saft-smiling gloaming,—
　　Yet the Green round the Cross-stane was empty and mute.

To the yellow-flower'd meadow and scant rigs o' tillage
　　The sheep a' neglected had come frae the glen;
The cushat-dow coo'd in the midst o' the village,
　　And the swallow had flown to the dwellings o' men!

—Sweet Denholm! not thus, when I lived in thy bosom,
　　Thy heart lay so still the last night o' the week;
Then nane was sae weary that love would nae rouse him,
　　And grief gaed to dance with a laugh on his cheek.

Sic thoughts wet my eyne—as the moonshine was beaming
　　On the kirk-tower that rose up sae silent and white;
The wan ghastly light on the dial was streaming,
　　But the still finger tauld not the hour o' the night.

Scene IV.   THE CITY OF THE PLAGUE.

The mirk-time past slowly in siching and weeping,
   I waken'd and nature lay silent in mirth;
Owr'e a' holy Scotland the Sabbath was sleeping,
   And heaven in beauty came down on the earth.

The morning smiled on—but nae kirk-bell was ringing,
   Nae plaid or blue bonnet came down frae the hill;
The kirk-door was shut, but nae psalm-tune was singing,
   And I miss'd the wee voices sae sweet and sae shrill.

I look'd owr'e the quiet o' Death's empty dwelling,
   The lav'rock walk'd mute 'mid the sorrowful scene,
And fifty brown hillocks wi' fresh mould were swelling
   Owre the kirk-yard o' Denholm last simmer sae green.

The infant had died at the breast o' its mither;
   The cradle stood still near the mitherless bed;
At play the bairn sunk in the hand o' its brither;
   At the fauld on the mountain the shepherd lay dead.

Oh! in spring time 'tis eerie, when winter is over,
   And birds should be glinting ow're forest and lea,
When the lint-white and mavis the yellow leaves cover,
   And nae blackbird sings loud frae the tap o' his tree.

But eerier far when the spring-land rejoices
   And laughs back to heaven with gratitude bright,
To hearken! and nae whare hear sweet human voices!
   When man's soul is dark in the season o' light!

Master of Revels. We thank thee, sweet one! for thy
   mournful song.

It seems, in the olden time, this very Plague
Visited thy hills and vallies, and the voice
Of lamentation wail'd along the streams
That now flow on through their wild paradise,
Murmuring their songs of joy. All that survive
In memory of that melancholy year
When died so many brave and beautiful,
Are some sweet mournful airs, some shepherd's lay
Most touching in simplicity, and none
Fitter to make one sad amid his mirth
Than the tune yet faintly singing through our souls.

Mary Gray. O! that I ne'er had sung it but at home
Unto my aged parents! to whose ear
Their Mary's tones were always musical.
I hear my own self singing o'er the moor,
Beside my native cottage,—most unlike
The voice which Edward Walsingham has prais'd,
It is the angel-voice of innocence.

2d Woman. I thought this cant were out of fashion now.
But it is well; there are some simple souls,
Even yet, who melt at a frail maiden's tears,
And give her credit for sincerity.
She thinks her eyes quite killing while she weeps.
Thought she as well of smiles, her lips would pout
With a perpetual simper. Walsingham
Hath prais'd these crying beauties of the north,
So whimpering is the fashion. How I hate
The dim dull yellow of that Scotish hair!

Scene IV. THE CITY OF THE PLAGUE.

Master of Revels. Hush! hush!—is that the sound of
   wheels I hear?
      [*The Dead-cart passes by, driven by a Negro.*]
Ha! dost thou faint, Louisa! one had thought
That railing tongue bespoke a mannish heart.
But so it ever is. The violent
Are weaker than the mild, and abject fear
Dwells in the heart of passion. Mary Gray,
Throw water on her face. She now revives.

Mary Gray. O sister of my sorrow and my shame!
Lean on my bosom. Sick must be your heart
After a fainting-fit so like to death.

Louisa, (recovering.) I saw a horrid demon in my
   dream!
With sable visage and white-glaring eyes,
He beckon'd on me to ascend a cart
Fill'd with dead bodies, muttering all the while
An unknown language of most dreadful sounds.
What matters it? I see it was a dream.
—Pray did the dead-cart pass?

Young Man.   Come, brighten up
Louisa! Though this street be all our own,
A silent street that we from death have rented,
Where we may hold our orgies undisturb'd,
You know those rumbling wheels are privileged,
And we must bide the nuisance. Walsingham,
To put an end to bickering, and these fits

D

Of fainting that proceed from female vapours,
Give us a song;—a free and gladsome song;
None of those Scottish ditties fram'd of sighs,
But a true English Bacchanalian song,
By toper chaunted o'er the flowing bowl.

 Master of Revels. I have none such; but I will sing a
  song
Upon the Plague. I made the words last night,
After we parted: a strange rhyming-fit
Fell on me; 'twas the first time in my life.
But you shall have it, though my vile crack'd voice
Wo'nt mend the matter much.

 Many voices.   A song on the Plague!
A song on the Plague! Let's have it! bravo! bravo!

SONG.

 Two navies meet upon the waves
 That round them yawn like op'ning graves;
 The battle rages; seamen fall,
 And overboard go one and all!
 The wounded with the dead are gone;
 But Ocean drowns each frantic groan,
 And, at each plunge into the flood,
 Grimly the billow laughs with blood.
 —Then, what although our Plague destroy
 Seaman and landman, woman, boy?
 When the pillow rests beneath the head,
 Like sleep he comes, and strikes us dead.
 What though into yon Pit we go,
 Descending fast, as flakes of snow?

Scene IV.   THE CITY OF THE PLAGUE.   51

What matters body without breath?
No groan disturbs that hold of death.

Chorus.
Then, leaning on this snow-white breast,
I sing the praises of the Pest!
If me thou would'st this night destroy,
Come, smite me in the arms of Joy.

Two armies meet upon the hill;
They part, and all again is still.
No! thrice ten thousand men are lying
Of cold, and thirst, and hunger dying.
While the wounded soldier rests his head,
About to die upon the dead,
What shrieks salute yon dawning light?
'Tis Fire that comes to aid the Fight!
—All whom our Plague destroys by day,
His chariot drives by night away.
And sometimes o'er a church-yard wall
His banner hangs, a sable pall!
Where in the light by Hecate shed
With grisly smile he counts the dead,
And piles them up a trophy high
In honour of his victory.
             Then leaning, &c.

King of the aisle! and church-yard cell!
Thy regal robes become thee well.
With yellow spots, like lurid stars
Prophetic of throne-shattering wars,
Bespangled is its night-like gloom,
As it sweeps the cold damp from the tomb.

Thy hand doth grasp no needless dart,
One finger touch benumbs the heart.
If thy stubborn victim will not die,
Thou roll'st around thy bloodshot eye,
And Madness leaping in his chain
With giant buffet smites the brain,
Or Idiocy with drivelling laugh
Holds out her strong-drugg'd bowl to quaff,
And down the drunken wretch doth lie
Unsheeted in the cemetery.
    Then leaning, &c.

Thou! Spirit of the burning breath
Alone deserv'st the name of Death!
Hide Fever! hide thy scarlet brow;
Nine days thou linger'st o'er thy blow,
Till the leach bring water from the spring,
And scare thee off on drenched wing.
Consumption! waste away at will!
In warmer climes thou fail'st to kill,
And rosy Health is laughing loud
As off thou steal'st with empty shroud!
Ha! blundering Palsy! thou art chill!
But half the man is living still;
One arm, one leg, one cheek, one side
In antic guise thy wrath deride.
But who may 'gainst thy power rebel,
King of the aisle! and church-yard cell.
    Then leaning, &c.

To Thee O Plague! I pour my song,
Since thou art come I wish thee long!

Thou strik'st the lawyer 'mid his lies,
The priest 'mid his hypocrisies.
The miser sickens at his hoard,
And the gold leaps to its rightful lord.
The husband, now no longer tied,
May wed a new and blushing bride,
And many a widow slyly weeps
O'er the grave where her old dotard sleeps,
While love shines through her moisten'd eye
On yon tall stripling gliding by.
'Tis ours who bloom in vernal years
To dry the love-sick maiden's tears,
Who turning from the relics cold,
In a new swain forgets the old.
Then leaning, &c.

Enter an old grey-headed Priest.

Priest. O impious table! spread by impious hands!
Mocking with feast and song and revelry
The silent air of death that hangs above it,
A canopy more dismal than the Pall!
Amid the church-yard darkness as I stood
Beside a dire interment, circled round
By the white ghastly faces of despair,
That hideous merriment disturb'd the grave,
And with a sacrilegious violence
Shook down the crumbling earth upon the bodies
Of the unsheeted dead. But that the prayers
Of holy age and female piety
Did sanctify that wide and common grave,

I could have thought that hell's exulting fiends
With shouts of devilish laughter dragg'd away
Some harden'd atheist's soul unto perdition.

    Several voices. How well he talks of hell! Go on, old
        boy!
The devil pays his tithes—yet he abuses him.

    Priest. Cease, I conjure you, by the blessed blood
Of Him who died for us upon the Cross,
These most unnatural orgies. As ye hope
To meet in heaven the souls of them ye lov'd,
Destroy'd so mournfully before your eyes,
Unto your homes depart.

    Master of Revels.   Our homes are dull—
And youth loves mirth.

    Priest.   O Edward Walsingham!
Art thou that groaning pale-fac'd man of tears
Who three weeks since knelt by thy mother's corpse,
And kiss'd the solder'd coffin, and leapt down
With rage-like grief into the burial vault,
Crying upon it's stone to cover thee
From this dim darken'd world? Would she not weep,
Weep even in heaven, could she behold her son
Presiding o'er unholy revellers,
And tuning that sweet voice to frantic songs
That should ascend unto the throne of grace
'Mid sob-broken words of prayer!

    Young Man.   Why! we can pray
Without a priest—pray long and fervently
Over the brimming bowl. Hand him a glass.

Master of Revels. Treat his grey hairs with reve-
    rence.
Priest.   Wretched boy!
This white head must not sue to thee in vain!
Come with the guardian of thy infancy,
And by the hymns and psalms of holy men
Lamenting for their sins, we will assuage
This fearful mirth akin to agony,
And in its stead, serene as the hush'd face
Of thy dear sainted parent, kindle hope
And heavenly resignation. Come with me.
    Young Man. They have a design against the hundredth
        Psalm.
Oh! Walsingham will murder cruelly
" All people that on earth do dwell."
Suppose we sing it here—I know the drawl.
    *Master of Revels, (silencing him, and addressing the
Priest.)* Why cam'st thou hither to disturb me thus?
I may not, must not go! Here am I held
By hopelessness in dark futurity,
By dire remembrance of the past,—by hatred
And deep contempt of my own worthless self,—
By fear and horror of the lifelessness
That reigns throughout my dwelling,—by the new
And frantic love of loud-tongued revelry,—
By the blest poison mantling in this bowl,—
And, help me Heaven! by the soft balmy kisses
Of this lost creature, lost, but beautiful

Even in her sin; nor could my mother's ghost
Frighten me from this fair bosom. 'Tis too late!
I hear thy warning voice—I know it strives
To save me from perdition, body and soul.
Beloved old man, go thy way in peace,
But curst be these feet if they do follow thee.

   Several Voices. Bravo! bravissimo! Our noble president!

Done with that sermonizing—off—off—off.

   Priest. Matilda's sainted spirit calls on thee!

   Master of Revels, (starting distractedly from his seat)
Didst thou not swear, with thy pale wither'd hands
Lifted to Heaven, to let that doleful name
Lie silent in the tomb for evermore?
O that a wall of darkness hid this sight
From her immortal eyes! She my betrothed
Once thought my spirit lofty, pure, and free,
And on my bosom felt herself in Heaven.
What am I now? *(looking up)*—O holy child of light,
I see thee sitting where my fallen nature
Can never hope to soar!

   Female Voice.   The fit is on him.
Fool! thus to rave about a buried wife!
See! how his eyes are fix'd.

   Master of Revels.   Most glorious star!
Thou art the spirit of that bright Innocent!
And there thou shinest with upbraiding beauty

On him whose soul hath thrown at last away
Not the hope only, but the wish of Heaven.
   Priest. Come, Walsingham!
   Master of Revels.   O holy father! go.
For mercy's sake, leave me to my despair.
   Priest. Heaven pity my dear son. Farewell! farewell!
               [*The Priest walks mournfully away.*]
   Young Man. Sing him another song. See how he turns
His eyes from yon far Heaven to Mary's bosom!
The man's in love. Ho! Walsingham! what cheer?
   Master of Revels, (angrily.) I hate that Irish slang—
it grates my soul.
   Mary Gray. O Walsingham! I fear to touch the breast
Where one so pure has lain! Yet turn thine eyes
Towards me, a sinful creature, that thy soul
May lose the sight of that celestial phantom
Whose beauty is a torment. List to me.
   Master of Revels. Here, Mary! with a calm deliberate soul
I swear to love thee! with such love, sweet girl!
As a man sunk in utter wretchedness
May cherish for a daughter of despair.
O maudlin fools! who preach of Chastity,
And call her Queen of Virtues! In the breast
Even of this prostitute (why should I fear

That word of three unmeaning syllables?)
In spite of all that's whisper'd from the grave,
I now will seek, and seeking I will find
The open-ey'd sleep of troubled happiness.

Mary Gray. All names are one to me. I often love
The imprecations of brutality,
Because, with vain contrition for my sins,
I feel that I deserve them all. But thou
Killest me with thy pitying gentleness,
Wasting sweet looks, and words of amity,
On a polluted creature drench'd in shame.

Young Man. Had yon old dotard, with his surplice on,
Emblem of his pretended sanctity,
And sanctimonious visage common to all
The hypocritic brotherhood of priests,
Staid but a little longer, I had read him
A lecture on the Christian's outworn creed.
This is rare season for the jugglery
Of these church-mountebanks!

Master of Revels. Fool! hold thy peace!
Thou in thy heart hast said there is no God,
Yet knowest thyself—a liar.

Young Man, (starting up furiously.) On his knees,
Upon his knees must Edward Walsingham
Implore forgiveness for these villanous words,
Or through his heart this sword will find a passage,
Even swifter than the Plague.

Master of Revels.   Upon my knees!
Fierce gladiator! dost thou think to daunt me
By that red rapier reeking with the blood
Of nerveless, hot-brain'd, inexperienc'd boys
Whom thou hast murder'd? Stand upon thy guard,
And see if all the skill of fencing France,
Or thy Italian practice, cowardly bravo!
Can ward this flash of lightning from thine eyes.

Enter FRANKFORT *and* WILMOT, *who rush between them.*

Frank. Madmen! put up your swords. What, Wal-
          singham!
The captain of the Ocean Queen, engag'd
In brawls on shore.

Master of Revels. Aye! 'tis a foolish quarrel,
And may have foolish ending: But he spake
With rude licentious tongue irreverently
Of a white head that since my mother's death
Hath been to me the holiest thing on earth;
And woe! to its blasphemer.

Young Man whispers.   St Martin's Fields,
At twelve o'clock. There is good moonlight for us.

Master of Revels. 'Tis a right hour. I'll meet thee
          at the elm-tree
Nam'd from the royal deer. At twelve o'clock!
                              [*The party breaks up.*]
What news from sea?

Frank. All well.

Master of Revels. Why look so pale?
Before an action fearless men look pale,
And fling away their smiles; but, once engag'd,
They scoff at death with gleesome mockery.
No deck was e'er so strew'd with hideous slaughter,
As the wide floor of this Plague-conquer'd city,
Therefore look up—our colours still are flying—
Will Frankfort strike them?

Frank. Yes! I am a coward!
I have for hours been wandering through this city,
And now I stand within a little furlong
Of the house that was my mother's. I have linger'd
In places quite remote—have travers'd streets
That led not thither—yea! have turn'd my face
Away from the imag'd dwelling of my parent,
Glad to put off the moment that might tell me
That which with agony I long to know.
Besides, mayhap, I am intruding here.
Good evening Walsingham—to you fair dames
Farewell. Come, Wilmot, o'er yon roof I see
The vane upon the house-top, where——

Walsingham. Your mother
On Thursday was alive.

Frank. God bless thee, Walsingham!
On Thursday—and 'tis yet but Sabbath-night.
She must be living still! Said they the Plague
Destroys so suddenly? In three small hours?

Three days and nights contain a frightful sum
Of fatal hours. The Plague doth ask but three—
She may be sick—dead—buried—and forgotten.

END OF THE FIRST ACT.

THE
CITY OF THE PLAGUE.

ACT II.

SCENE I.

The street opposite a house adjoining Aldgate church-yard.

Frank. Hush, Wilmot! while I say one little pray'r.
There stands the house—I see it in my soul,
Though yet mine eyes dare not to look on it.
—Let me lean on thee—hear'st thou aught within?

Wil. It is the hour of rest: I nothing hear;
But the house methinks is slumb'ring happily
In the clear moon-light. 'Tis a lovely night,
Beauty without these walls, and peace within.

Frank. Wears it the look of a deserted dwelling?

Wil. Its silence seems of sleep and not of death.

Frank. O Wilmot! sure the moon shines ruefully,
On these black windows faintly ting'd with light!
I see no difference between these dark walls,
And yonder tomb-stones—they both speak of death.

Wil. Be comforted.

Frank. List! Wilmot! hear'st thou aught?
Methinks it was my mother's voice within
Singing a dirge-like hymn. Hear'st thou a voice?

Wil. Grief mocks itself with fancied sounds like these;
There was no voice.

Frank. O let it breathe again,
And all the world will seem alive to me.
—O God! the silence of this lifeless street,
Where all the human dwellings stand like tombs
Empty or fill'd with corpses, seems collected
Round this one house, whose shadowy glimmering walls
Bear down my soul in utter hopelessness.
Oh! 'tis a sad, sad wreck. Mark how the dust
Lies on th' untrodden steps! and yet I see
Footprints of one ascending. As I live,
I hear a footstep in my mother's chamber.
A light! a light! see where a light is moving
As from an apparition through the house.

[*The door opens, and the Priest who appeared in the first Act comes into the street.*]

Frank. Pale death is in his troubled countenance.
The house is falling from me, and the street
Is sinking down—down—down. I faint—Support me.

The Priest. [*To* W<small>IL</small>. *while they support* F<small>RANK</small>.]
At a sad hour the sailor hath return'd.
Would he were yet at sea.

Frank. I hear thy voice,
And know that I indeed am motherless.

Priest. Blessed are they who lived in the Lord,
And in the Lord did die.
   Frank.   Amen—amen!
Hath little William gone with her to Heaven?
   Priest. They died few hours apart. Methought I
     saw
The angelical mother smiling up the sky
With that delightful infant on her breast,
More like a spirit that had come from Heaven
To waft away the child to Paradise,
Than a human soul departing from this earth.
   Frank. Soaring in beauty to immortal bliss!
But away from him who held them in his heart,
An everlasting presence of delight
'Mid the dim dreary sea.
   Priest.   Weep, weep my son,
I wish to see thee weep.
   Frank.   O why should tears
Be shed unto the blest and beautiful
By us poor dwellers in the woeful shades
Of mortal being?
   Wil.   Thou art deadly pale!
Be not asham'd to weep upon my breast.
I have seen thee weeping for that sweet child's sake
When haply he was dancing in his mirth——
   Frank. Dancing in his mirth! The lovely child is
     dead.
All all his innocent thoughts like rose-leaves scattered,

And his glad childhood nothing but a dream!
I feel his last kiss yet—— *(weeping.)*

Wil.   I also weep—
For I too am his brother, though his face
Was only vision'd sweetly in my soul
With its small features——

Frank.   Sudden happiness
Comes o'er my grief! Time and this world appear
Mere shadows, and I feel as if I stood
Close to my mother's side!—O mournful weakness!
The realms of Heaven are stretching far away;
My soul is fetter'd to the earth; the grave
Cries with a voice that may not be gainsay'd,
And mortal life appears eternity,
Since she I lov'd has perish'd.

Priest.   Some, my son,
Would bid thee trust in time, the friend of sorrow;
But thou hast nobler comforters; nor would I
Bid thee place hope in blind forgetfulness.
I know that there is taken from thy soul
Something that must return no more—a joy
That from the shore breath'd on thee far at sea,
Filling thy heart with home; and sweeter far
Arose that feeling o'er the ocean-calm
Than airs balsamic breathing through the ship
From odorous island unseen 'mid the waves.

Frank. O kind old man! Thy sweet and solemn
    voice,

Fit organ for such peaceful images,
Breathes a calm reconcilement through my soul.
These silvery locks made white by time and sorrow,
Yet in their reverend beauty meekly smiling
At what hath made them so, most silently
Inspire my heart although yet young in grief,
With resignation almost like thine own.

 Priest. Son! hast thou strength to look upon that sight
Where human loveliness seems perfected
By the last smile that will not pass away?

 Frank. They yet then are unburied?

 Priest.   Even this day,
At the hour when yonder bell would have been tolling,
In other times than these, for morning-service,
Her spirit went to heaven—your brother died
Some little hours before.

 Frank.   And in that house
My mother and her little son lie dead!
—Yes! I have strength to look on them,—to kiss
Their cold white faces—to embrace their bodies
Though soul be gone still tenderly beloved,—
To gaze upon their eyelids, though the light
Must never break in beauty from below them,
And, with the words of fondest agony,
Softly to whisper love unto the ear
That in its frozen silence hears me not.

 Priest. I will conduct thee to them.

Frank.   At the hour
When she was dying, in our vessel's barge
Was I approaching to the shore,—the oars
Sounded as they were muffled on the black
And sluggish water! 'Twas a gloomy hour,
Yet, dark as it was, I ne'er expected this.
One visit will I pay them e'er I go.
Oh! I have many a heavy thought to utter
Which God alone must hear.
    Priest.   We will pray for thee,
Standing uncover'd in this silent street.
And when we think thy soul is satisfied
With the awful converse holden with the dead,
We will come to thee for a little while,
And sit with thee beside their bodies. God
Will not forsake thee in this last distress.
    Frank. I dare not enter, though I yearn to lie
For ever by their side. The very beauty
Which in their sleeping faces I shall see
With its fair image holds me motionless.
A gulf of darkness lies beyond that door!
—O tell me, reverend father! how they died,
And haply then I may have strength to go
And see them dead:—Now 'tis impossible.
Wilmot! why do you weep—be comforted.
    Priest. Though from the awful suddenness of their death
The Plague hath surely stricken them, yet they lie

Unlike the other victims of that pest
In more than mortal beauty. Their still faces,
When last I saw them, in the moonlight lay,
Like innocence sleeping in the love of heaven,
Love mix'd with pity. Though a smile was there,
It seem'd a smile ne'er meant for human eye,
Nor seem'd regarding me; but there it shone,
A mournful lustre filling all the room
With the silence of its placid holiness.

Frank. Lovelier than when alive they might not be.
Tell how they died.

Priest.   Last night I sat with her
And talk'd of thee;—two tranquil hours we talk'd
Of thee and none beside, while little William
Sat in his sweet and timid silent way
Upon his stool beside his mother's knees,
And, sometimes looking upwards to her face,
Seem'd listening of his brother far at sea.
This morning early I look'd in upon them
Almost by chance. There little William lay
With his bright hair and rosy countenance
Dead! though at first I thought he only slept.
" You think," his mother said, " that William sleeps!
" But he is dead! He sicken'd during the night,
" And while I pray'd he drew a long deep sigh,
" And breath'd no more!"

Frank.   O sweet and sinless child!
Go on—go on!

Priest.   I look'd on her who spake,
And I saw something in her tearless eyes
More than a mother's grief—the cold dull gleam
Of mortal sickness hastening to decay.
She ask'd me not to leave her, and I staid
Till human help or comfort by that saint
No more was needed. But a gentler death
A Christian never died. Methought her soul
Faded in light, even as a glorious star
Is hidden 'mid the splendours of the morn.

Frank. I hope she wept not long and bitterly
For her poor sailor's sake. O cruel wind
That kept our ship last night far out at sea!

Priest. " In life I was most happy in my son,"
She said, " and none may know the happiness
" His image yields me at the hour of death."
—I found that she had laid upon her bed
Many of those little presents that you brought her
From your first voyage to the Indies. Shells
With a sad lustre brighten'd o'er the whiteness
Of these her funeral sheets; and gorgeous feathers,
With which, few hours before, her child was playing,
And lisping all the while his brother's name,
Form'd a sad contrast with the pale, pale face
Lying so still beneath its auburn hair.
Two letters still are in her death-closed hand
And will be buried with her. One was written
By your captain, after the great victory

Over De Ruyter, and with loftiest praise
Of her son's consummate skill and gallantry
During the battle, told how he had saved
The lives of two young noble Hollanders,
By leaping overboard amid a storm.
The other, now almost effaced by tears,
Was from yourself, the last she had from you,
And spoke of your return.   God bless thee boy!
I am too old to weep—but such return
Wrings out the tears from my old wither'd heart.

Frank. O 'tis the curse of absence that our love
Becomes too sad—too tender—too profound
Towards all our far-off friends.   Home we return
And find them dead for whom we often wept,
Needlessly wept when they were in their joy!
Then goes the broken-hearted mariner
Back to the sea that welters drearily
Around the homeless earth!

Priest.   Thy mother waits
Her son's approach—in beauty and in peace.

Frank. I go into her chamber—fear me not.
I will not rush into the holy presence
With frantic outcry, and with violent steps
Most unbecoming 'mid the hush of death.
But I, with footsteps gentle as the dew,
And with suspended breath, will reach her bed;
There silent as she is, so will I be,

Lying beside my mother in her sleep
With my head upon her bosom—cold—cold—cold.

SCENE II.

A little room in a lonely street in the suburbs.—Isabel *sitting with the Bible on her knees.*—*Enter* Magdalene.

Isabel. My gracious lady bless that face again!
Here have I sat this long, long wretched day
Quite by myself, until I thought with horror
You never might return.

Magd.   O needless fears!
Sister! thy anxious heart will never learn
To think more on thyself, and less on others.
Yet to thy friends thine are endearing faults
And make thee lov'd the more.

Isabel.   How pale you look!
Wearied, and pale, and languid—sit down here
My gentle mistress! Blest is charity
From ordinary hands, but sure from thine
It must drop on the children of the poor,
Like dew from heaven upon th' unconscious lambs.

Magd. I will sit down a while. I have been kept
From home, beyond my promis'd hour, by sad
And unexpected duty. Frankfort's mother,
And her sweet little son, this morning died.

Isabel. Both dead! I might have known it from that
face.

Magd. I have prepared their bodies for the grave,
And with such flowers as in a desert-square
Of the city I could gather, are they drest,
Sleeping together sound and silently.

Isabel. O what will that kind-hearted sailor think,
When he returns from sea!

Magd. I shudder for him,
His love was so profound.

Isabel. O matchless pair!
In love, in beauty, and in innocence
So long united, now your orphan hearts
Will closer cling in your calamity;
As I have seen upon a leafless bough
Two young doves sitting silent, breast to breast.

Magd. Happy may he be for ever—may his ship
Linger in friendly port, or far at sea
Be chain'd in long, long calm, so that he comes not
Unto this city of the Plague! He lives,
And long will live—that thought is happiness
Enough for me. I see him on the deck,
Walking and speaking——O good Isabel!
A bright and sunny vision often breaks
Upon my praying soul, even at the bed
Where death is busy, and with contrite heart
I strive to dim it: Angel-like it is,

But oh! too dear in its humanity,
And, like a spirit lingering round a tomb,
It ever haunts my desolated bosom.

Isabel. Cherish that image—he will yet return
To live with thee for ever.

Magd.   Noble spirit!
I thought I lov'd him well when we were happy,
And liv'd together 'mid all happy things,
As of our bliss partaking. Death has come
And in affection left us parentless;
And now it seems that all the love I bore
My father and my mother has been pour'd
Into that mild, that brave, that generous heart.
Aye! what will he say indeed when he returns!

Isabel. Thy parents both are dead—one month ago
They died before thine eyes, yet where on earth
Might we behold a countenance array'd
In the light of an immortal happiness
O Magdalene! like to thine?

Madg.   Sometimes I fear
I have a stony heart.

Isabel.   The hush thou feel'st
Will breathe through Frankfort's soul on his return,
And you will speak together of the dead
As of some gentle beings, who have gone
To sojourn in a far-off happy land
Which one day ye will visit.

Madg.   I know well

That they who love their friends most tenderly
Still bear their loss the best. There is in love
A consecrated power, that seems to wake
Only at the touch of death from its repose
In the profoundest depths of thinking souls.
Superior to the outward signs of grief,
Sighing or tears,—when these have past away,
It rises calm and beautiful, like the moon
Saddening the solemn night, yet with that sadness
Mingling the breath of undisturbed peace.

   Isabel. With that sublime faith ye will both be happy.

   Madg. How bright and fair that afternoon returns
When last we parted. Even now I feel
Its dewy freshness in my soul! Sweet breeze!
That hymning like a spirit up the lake
Came through the tall pines on yon little isle
Across to us upon the vernal shore
With a kind friendly greeting. Frankfort blest
The unseen musician floating through the air,
And smiling said, " Wild harper of the hill!
" So may'st thou play thy ditty when once more
" This lake I do revisit." As he spoke,
Away died the music in the firmament,
And unto silence left our parting hour.
No breeze will ever steal from nature's heart
So sweet again to me.

   Isabel.   Can'st thou not think
Of e'er again returning to the vale

Where we were born. Should Frankfort come from sea
Thou art his own betrothed: two such souls
Are not by God destin'd to live apart
Even on this earth, and e'er you go to heaven
To join the blessed dead whom we deplore,
They would regard your life of sanctity
From their bright courts with joy, and your still walks
Through vale and forest by those holy watchers
Be kept from earthly ill.

Madg.   Whate'er my doom,
It cannot be unhappy. God hath given me
The boon of resignation: I could die,
Though doubtless human fears would cross my soul,
Calmly even now;—yet if it be ordain'd
That I return unto my native valley
And live with Frankfort there, why should I fear
To say I might be happy—happier far
Than I deserve to be. Sweet Rydal lake!
Am I again to visit thee? to hear
Thy glad waves murmuring all around my soul?

Isabel. Methinks I see us in a cheerful groupe
Walking along the margin of the bay
Where our lone summer-house......

Madg.   Sweet mossy cell!
So cool—so shady—silent and compos'd!
A constant evening full of gentle dreams!
Where joy was felt like sadness, and our grief
A melancholy pleasant to be borne.

Hath the green linnet built her nest this spring
In her own rose-bush near the quiet door?
Bright solitary bird! she oft will miss
Her human friends: Our orchard now must be
A wilderness of sweets, by none belov'd.

Isabel. One blessed week would soon restore its beauty,
Were we at home. Nature can work no wrong.
The very weeds how lovely! the confusion
Doth speak of breezes, sunshine, and the dew.

Madg. I hear the murmuring of a thousand bees
In that bright odorous honeysuckle wall
That once enclos'd the happiest family
That ever lived beneath the blessed skies.
Where is that family now? O Isabel,
I feel my soul descending to the grave,
And all these loveliest rural images
Fade, like waves breaking on a dreary shore.

Isabel. Even now I see a stream of sunshine bathing
The bright moss-roses round our parlour window!
Oh! were we sitting in that room once more!

Madg. 'Twould seem inhuman to be happy there
And both my parents dead. How could I walk
On what I used to call my father's walk,
He in his grave! or look upon that tree
Each year so full of blossoms or of fruit
Planted by my mother, and her holy name
Graven on its stem by mine own infant hands!

Isabel. It would be haunted, but most holy ground.

Madg. How tenderly did Frankfort love my parents!
From the first hour we met, his image seem'd
In the still bosom of our family
The silent picture of an absent friend!
—Methinks I hear his voice while he recites
Some fragment of a poem, or wild song
About the troubles of the pitiless sea.
Most other sailors have loud jocund voices;
But his was always low and somewhat sad
As if he bore within his soul the sound
Of that wild-raging world, the memory
Of battle and of shipwreck, and of friends
By death ta'en from him or captivity.

 Isabel. Much hath that brave man suffer'd, yet he
  pities
All them who mourn—nor on himself bestows
So much as one sad dream.

 Magd.   Dost thou remember
That melancholy but delightful strain
He framed one summer evening in our cell,
When that fair orphan came with streaming eyes,
To tell us that the lady of the castle
Marie Le Fleming on her death-bed lay?

 Isabel. I recollect it well.

 Magd.   The sorrowful
Still love to muse on all distressing things,
And sure her death was so. Repeat the dirge
Composed while she was parting from the earth.

E'er yet thy voice begin, I see the land,
The beautiful land of mountains, lakes, and woods,
All glimmering with a melancholy light
Which must unto mine eyes endure for ever.
O Isabel! when o'er this doleful city
Rises the snow-white tower of Grassmere church
——Go on,—go on, for I begin to rave.

DIRGE.

 The fairy on Helvellyn breathes
  Into the diamond's lustre fair,
 And in that magic gleam she wreathes
  The dew-drops round her glittering hair.

 The driving blast—the dimming rains
  May there disturb its secret place;
 But evermore the stone retains
  The image of that loveliest face.

 Into our lady's radiant eyes
  Joy look'd when she was yet a child,
 And there 'mid shades of sickness lies
  Beauteous as when at first she smil'd.

 —'Tis said there is a wond'rous bird
  That ne'er alights to fold her wings,
 But far up in the sky is heard
  The music which the creature sings.

 On plumes unwearied, soft and bright
  She floateth still in hymning mirth,

For ever in her native light!
  Unstain'd by any touch of earth!

Our lady's soft and gentle feet
  O'er earth in mortal motion swim,
But angels come from heaven to meet
  The incense of her holy hymn.

—On yonder pool so black and deep,
  In her green cradle rock'd to rest,
Behold the water-lily sleep!
  Serenely, with untroubled breast!

Alike unto that fearless flower
  The arrowy sleet—the dewy balm—
The sunlight's smile—the tempest's lower—
  For her's is an eternal calm.

Across our gracious lady's bed
  A blast hath come as from the grave,
But on her pillow rests her head
  Calm as that lily on the wave.

—From heaven fair beings come at night
  To watch o'er mortals while they sleep;
Angels are they, whose sole delight
  It is to comfort those who weep.

How softly on the dreamer's head
  They lay their soft and snow-white hands!
One smile! then in a moment fled,
  They melt away to happier lands.

I wake! and lo! my lady fair
    Is smiling near the orphan's bed—
With all the charms the living wear
    Join'd to the beauty of the dead.

—O perfect is a plaintive tune
    When slowly sung at fall of even,
In some wild glen beneath the moon,
    When silence binds the earth and heaven!

Remembrance rises faint and dim
    Of sorrows suffer'd long ago,
And joy delighteth in the hymn
    Although it only breathe of woe.

Our lady's spirit it is pure
    As music of departed years!
On earth too beauteous to endure,
    So sad—so wild—so full of tears!

Magd. Methinks I see the splendid funeral
O'erspreading Grassmere church-yard. Vain parade!
Lost on the thousand weepers standing there,
With the image of that corpse so beautiful
Lying all dress'd with flowers before their souls.
The ancient castle from that dismal day
Seem'd going fast to ruin—the oak-wood
Is black and sullen 'mid sunshiny hours,
And oft upon the green and primrose bank
Of her own Rydal lake, the voice of grief

Comes with the little waves, a peaceful dirge
Of Nature o'er the lady whom she lov'd.

 Isabel. Nature most gently led her unto rest.
And as her eyes grew dim, there swam before them
Sweet images of all that most she lov'd
Breath'd from the heavens and earth. O different far
Must be our doom! Hark! hark the nightly shrieks!
At the same stated hour! those thundering wheels!
Ah me! I never hear that hideous noise,
But the deep hush of Grassmere vale—the tower
Chiming through morning-silence, and the lake
Reflecting all the heavens——

 Magd.   Of this no more
My gentle Isabel! Can we speak so long
About ourselves, and Frankfort's mother lying
A corpse! It seems as if we had not loved her.
O we are selfish beings even when we think
That we have wean'd our souls from earthly joys.

 Isabel. When is the funeral?

 Magd.   At twelve o'clock
To-night will that delightful old man come,
To see them decently carried to the grave;
And I will in that small procession walk
Close to her dear, dear head. She was belov'd
By all who saw her once—so beautiful!
So meekly beautiful! so sadly fair!
So happy in her solemn widowhood!

Isabel. You will return at midnight ?

Magd.   Yes—kind heart !
And for one single day I must refrain
From visiting the sick. A trying day
Hath this been to me. O ye holy Ones,
With saints united in beatitude,
Look down upon us in this lonely room
Sitting in the dimness of mortality
With sorrow in our souls !—My Isabel,
I may not chaunt with thee our evening hymn,
For I am faint. Already have I pour'd
My heart in holy song unto the ear
Of pitying Jesus—sing it by thyself:
In silence will I join the sacred strain.

HYMN.

    The air of death breathes through our souls,
        The dead all round us lie ;
    By day and night the death-bell tolls
        And says " Prepare to die."

    The face that in the morning sun
        We thought so wond'rous fair,
    Hath faded, ere his course was run,
        Beneath its golden hair.

    I see the old man in his grave
        With thin locks silvery-grey ;
    I see the child's bright tresses wave
        In the cold breath of the clay.

The loving ones we lov'd the best,
  Like music all are gone!
And the wan moonlight bathes in rest
  Their monumental stone.

But not when the death-prayer is said,
  The life of life departs;
The body in the grave is laid,
  Its beauty in our hearts.

At holy midnight voices sweet
  Like fragrance fill the room,
And happy ghosts with noiseless feet
  Come bright'ning from the tomb.

We know who sends the visions bright,
  From whose dear side they came!
—We veil our eyes before thy light,
  We bless our Saviour's name!

This frame of dust, this feeble breath
  The Plague may soon destroy;
We think on Thee, and feel in death
  A deep and awful joy.

Dim is the light of vanish'd years
  In the glory yet to come;
O idle grief! O foolish tears!
  When Jesus calls us home.

Like children for some bauble fair
  That weep themselves to rest;
We part with life—awake! and there
  The jewel in our breast!

SCENE III.

The open street.—A crowd of men and women gathered together in a tumultuous manner.

1st Man. There goes a notable fool! The moon is
        yonder
Shining like the sun, but with a tamer light,
And yet with blazing oil-torch puffing forth
Its noisome vapours on each passenger,
This greasy varlet scours along the street,
Fixing his puny stars where'er he stops,
In many a long line twinkling sleepily.
What is the use of these same lamps? The Plague
Is not afraid of light, and kills by day,
By moonlight, star-light, lamp-light, every light.
Is it that we may see each others faces
More clearly as we pass? Now on my soul
I have not seen one face for these three months
That spoke not of the grave. This very wretch,
With long lean shrivell'd shanks, look'd as he pass'd
Like some well season'd dry anatomy
Escap'd from Surgeons'-hall. The Plague, my girl,
Hath spoil'd the beauties of good London town,
And, (let me see thy face below this lamp)
Good faith! they're not so useless as I thought—
Had'st thou been Eve, Adam had ne'er been tempted.

2d Man. Aye! folks may jest, and with right heavy
　　　　　hearts.
For my own part, I don't expect this Plague
Will change its quarters, long as it has left
A single man alive. As for the moon
That shines so brightly, have you ever heard
What the Astrologers say of that moon?
Woman. Tell, tell us what the Astrologers have said.
2d Man. They say it is the moon that sends the
　　　　　Plague.
1st Man. The man in the moon? then is he chang'd
　　　　　indeed
Since days of yore. I have seen him when a boy
Crouching beneath his sticks most woefully,
Condemn'd to bear the load in punishment
Of Sabbath-breaking. Now he walks erect
With a huge sweeping scythe, and mows us down,
Us poor unhappy Londoners, like grass
By the acre.
3d Man. Yea! before the Plague burst out,
All who had eye-sight witness'd in the city
Dread Apparitions, that sent through the soul
Forebodings of some wild calamity.
The very day-light seem'd not to be pour'd
Down from the sun—a ghastly glimmering haze
Sent upwards from the earth; while every face
Look'd wan and sallow gliding through the streets
That echoed in the darkness. When the veil

Of mist was drawn aside, there hung the sun
In the unrejoicing atmosphere, blood-red,
And beamless in his wrath. At morn and even,
And through the dismal day, that fierce aspect
Glar'd on the City, and many a wondering groupe
Gaz'd till they scarce believ'd it was the sun.
—Did any here behold, as I beheld,
That Phantom who three several nights appear'd,
Sitting upon a cloud-built throne of state
Right o'er St Paul's Cathedral? On that throne
At the dead hour of night he took his seat,
And monarch-like stretch'd out his mighty arm
That shone like lightning. In that kingly motion
There seem'd a steadfast threat'ning—and his features,
Gigantic 'neath their shadowy diadem,
Frown'd, as the Phantom vow'd within his heart
Perdition to the City. Then he rose,
Majestic spectre! keeping still his face
Towards the domes beneath, and disappear'd,
Still threatening with his outstretch'd arm of light,
Into a black abyss behind the clouds.

Voice from the crowd. I saw him—on the very night
  I saw him,
When first the Plague broke out.

3d Man.   And saw ye not
The sheeted corpses stalking through the sky
In long long troops together—yet all silent,
And unobservant of each other, gliding

Down a dark flight of steps that seem'd to lead
Into the bosom of eternity?
    Voice from the crowd. Go on, go on—tell us of what
    thou sawest:
Thou art a scholar, and thy tongue can speak
Even like a written book. What sawest thou else?
    3d Man. I have seen hearses moving through the sky!
Not few or solitary, as on earth
They pass us by upon a lonesome road.
But thousands, tens of thousands mov'd along
In grim procession—a long league of plumes
Tossing in the storm that roar'd aloft in heaven,
Yet bearing onwards through the hurricane,
A black, a silent, a wild cavalcade
That nothing might restrain; till in a moment
The heavens were freed, and all the sparkling stars
Look'd through the blue and empty firmament!
    Voice. They all foretold the Plague.
    3d Man.   And I have seen
A mighty church-yard spread its dreary realms
O'er half the visible heavens—a church-yard blacken'd
With ceaseless funerals that besieg'd the gates
With lamentation and a wailing echo,
O'er that aërial cemet'ry hung a bell
Upon a black and thund'rous looking cloud,
And there at intervals it swung and toll'd
Throughout the startled sky! Not I alone,
But many thousands heard it—leaping up,

Not knowing whether it might be a dream,
As if an earthquake shook them from their beds,
Nor dar'd again to sleep.

1st Woman. Cease, cease that jargon
About sights seen in the sky. The city shews
Phantoms, and hearses, and church-yards enow,
Without recourse to visions in the heaven.

Voice. Heed not that foolish wretch—go on, go on,
I love to feel my hair stand up on end,
And my heart beat till I can hear its sound.

3d Man. Dost not remember that black stormy night,
When all at once the hurricano ceased,
And silence came as suddenly as light
Bursting on darkness? In that awful hush
The City like a panting monster lay,
Fearful of danger which it knew not of,
Yet felt that it was near. Then overhead,
As from a floating cloud, a mighty voice
Came like the roar of ocean " Death! death! death!"
A thousand echoes wail'd the giant-cry
Faintlier and faintlier—till once more the storm
Rose on the night, and that portentous voice
Left the pale city quaking in its fear.

2d Woman. His words are like a dream—more terrible
These sights and sounds from the disastrous sky
Than all the real terrors of the Plague.

1st Man. Come woman! with that wild and coal-black eye,

Let us hear thee speak! no idle dreamer thou!
I like that smile of scorn and bitterness.

   1st Woman. I cannot say that I dislike the Plague.
Good faith! it yields rare harvest to the poor
Who are industrious, and will sit by night
Round beds where richer servants dare not come.
Yet after all 'tis not the Plague that kills,
But Fear. A shake of the head—a sapient look—
Two or three ugly words mutter'd through the teeth—
Will go long way to send unto his grave
A soldier who has stood fire in his day.
And as for women, and the common run
Of men—for instance mercers, lawyers' clerks,
And others not worth mentioning, they die,
If a sick-nurse only look upon her watch
To know the hour o' the night? What matters it?
In a hundred years—all will be well again.

   2d Woman. You must have seen rare sights in your
      time, good woman!

   1st Woman. I have seen for two months past some
      score i' the day
Give up the ghost. No easy business
To lay so many out. When they paid well,
I did my office neatly—but the poor
Or niggardly, I put them overhand
In a somewhat careless way—gave them a stretch
Or two—down with their eye-lids—shut their mouths,
And so I left them. 'Twas but slovenly work,

Scene III.   THE CITY OF THE PLAGUE.   91

 2d Woman. Ha! ha! ha!—Why wert thou so kind,
   brave wench!
Unto the lazy cruel-hearted rich?
They owe at least one kindness to the poor.
Let them feel what still they preach of—gratitude.
 1st Woman. I know not what the gentry and nobility
Think of this way of burial. In they go,
Beggar and banker, porter, gentleman,
The cinder-wench and my white-handed lady
Into one pit. O rare! rare bed-fellows!
There they all lie in uncomplaining sleep.
 2d Woman. Can'st give some little history of the dead?
 1st Woman. Yes—I could make your pale face paler
   still,
Did I choose to be talkative—but one
Short history of a wretch who died to-day
I will give—and his name was Rivington.
Eternal curses blast that hateful name!—
Curst be he even within the crowded grave!
And may his lingering spirit feel the pressure
Of a hundred corpses weighing down its life,
In agony and torment down to hell.
 2d Woman. Come for the story—you may spare your
   curses.
God wot! you waste your breath. The gentleman
Is dead—I'll warrant that his soul's ta'en care of.
 1st Woman. I was sent for to a house that was plague-
   struck,

To lay out two small children. Rivington!
Methought I knew that name. Could it be he
Whom twenty years before I knew too well
Among the towers of Oxford, where he studied
As some said for the church; a worthy son
Of such a mother—no less worthy child
Of such a rare nurse—Oxford and the church!
At once I knew the caitiff, as he lay
Dying alone 'mid his dead family,
Whose blue-swollen faces had a look in them
Of their most wicked father. Had they liv'd,
They had been evil—no good could have come
From blood of his—it had a taint in it.
I had forgot to mention that his wife
Was likewise lying dead. Poor soul! her face
Was beautiful, and seem'd the face of sorrow
Rather than of death. Much no doubt had she suffer'd,
Married for ten long years to such a husband!
When I had done my duty, " Where's your gold?"
I ask'd this master of a family,
Who with a fix'd and stupid face was sitting
Idle in his chair. " Where ruffian! is your gold?"
But, to make short a rather tedious story,
He knew me—knew that I was come to curse him,
To howl my dying curses in his ear,
Nor would I listen to his cowardly voice
Imploring mercy and forgiveness. Curse him!

2d Woman. What was his crime?

Scene III.   THE CITY OF THE PLAGUE.   93

 1st Woman.   We were three sisters once
Happy and young, and some thought beautiful,
And by our cheerful industry supported
Our palsied mother. But this demon came,
And by his wheedling arts and tempting gold,
Unknown to one another we all fell
Into sin, and shame, and sorrow. Our sick mother
Died of a broken heart—one sister died
In childbed—and consumption bred of grief
Soon took away another. I alone,
Reserv'd for farther woe and wickedness,
Liv'd on—but yet methinks this one small day,
Those two blest hours in which I saw him dying,
That minute when the rattle in his throat
Clos'd his vile tongue for ever, and the moment
When one convulsive gasp left him a corpse,
Gave me my share of earthly happiness,
And life feels life thus sweeten'd by revenge.

 2d Woman. Felt you no little twinging of remorse,
Thinking on days when I suppose you lov'd him?

 1st Woman. I never lov'd him, and he knows what
  love
He bore to me. Both had our punishment!
I for my folly, vanity and pride,
Base love of gold (for then that love was base
Which now is right, and just, and necessary),
Have led a houseless life of infamy,
Despis'd, curst, fondled, starv'd. He for his lust,

Unnumber'd lies, and fearless cruelty,
Hath seen his children die before his face,
And his wife perish, stricken into death
'Mid the screaming of insanity. Remorse
Disturb'd his ruffled bed and dug his grave,
While she, within whose breast he often lay,
With the count'nance of a fury glar'd upon him,
And shook the dying caitiff in the pangs
Of pain and of despair. The hand of God
Was there in me its worthless instrument.

 2d Woman. Let's go to merry-making—right good
   friends
We two shall make. Left naked in the street
Was I, a little infant by its mother
Expos'd to death. I in a poor-house past
My hated, hateful youth; my womanhood
Like thine was chiefly past where I began
My chance-existence—in the street; and now
Without a friend, food, money or a home,
What care I for the Plague? Let us go my friend
To merry-making.

 1st Man. All this is mighty well,
But leads to nothing. Wilt thou rob a church
Good master Pale-face? Wilt thou rob a church,
And share 'mid this our ragged company
The general spoil?

 2d Man. Why any place but a church!

1st Man.   Ha! thou'rt a scrupulous robber! and the sound
Of these psalm-singing, shrill-voiced choristers
Would frighten thee gliding through the moonlight-aisle.
Troth man! 'tis well worth fighting with a ghost
For such a booty.   Silver candlesticks
Gold-gilt are standing idle on the altar,
Themselves a boy-load! and they say a Crozier
Most richly ornamented may be found
In a lucky nook,—no despicable bauble!
But ten times worth such trifles, think thou Jesuit!
On the bright vessels for communion-service,
Of massy silver, which the surpliced priest
With both hands gives unto the trembling grasp
Of young communicants.   When melted down
They will make us all as rich as Crœsus.   Come!
Let us off to the Cathedral.

2d Man.   I for one
Stay where I am, or seek some other duty.
'Tis absolute sacrilege.   I could not sleep
If I had lent a hand to rob a church.
I go not there to pray—neither will I go
To steal—'tis little short of sacrilege.
However I am not obstinate, and 'tis pity
To part from pleasant company—suppose
We break into some house that is plague-struck.
Its tenants probably are dead,—or dying,

And will make small resistance—to kill such
Cannot be well called murder.

Several voices.   Agreed! Agreed!
[*A wild cry is heard, and a half-naked man comes raving furiously along.*]

2d Man. 'Tis the mad Prophet! for God's sake let him pass.

Maniac. Woe! woe! unto the city! woe! woe! woe!
The Prince of the air his palace fills to-day
With wicked spirits in their guilt destroy'd.
Repent! repent! before the red-eyed Wrath
Wither you to ghosts. His bloody scymitar
Is waving o'er the city. On your knees
Fall down ye wild blasphemers!—'Tis too late,
Woe! woe! unto the city! woe! woe! woe!

2d Man. We neither rob a church nor house this night.

Maniac. Repent ye miserable troop of ghosts.

2d Man. We cannot repent—fear binds us fast to guilt.

Maniac. Another month, and I am left alone
In the vast city, shrieking like a demon!
Condemned to an eternal solitude
Peopled but by ghosts, that will not will not speak!
All gliding past me, wan and silently,
With curses in their eyes, and death-like frost
Breathed from their bony hands, whose scornful fingers
Keep pointing at me rooted to the stones,
That yield no sound to comfort my stopp'd heart.

Scene III.   THE CITY OF THE PLAGUE.   97

 Crowd. O what a dreadful dream envelopes him!
 Maniac. My sins have brought this judgment on the
  city.
One sin there is that may not be forgiven,
And that was mine: so from the lurid sky
Down came the mighty and the fearful God,
And like a flash of lightning wither'd up
The hearts of his poor creatures. I alone
Am doom'd to live for ever in the depths
Of lifeless silence, which my madden'd shrieks
In vain will startle, like a lonely bird
Wailing unheeded in a vast sea-cave.
—O Jesus! thou Destroyer! once again
Thy voice of thunder stuns me. Woe! woe! woe!
—The streets do run with blood! and groans of death
As with an earthquake shake the toppling walls.
Down falls yon spire—huzza! down, down to hell.
Why stare ye so, ye dumb and pale-fac'd ghosts?
O for a whirlwind's wing to sweep you away
Like broken clouds, or the autumnal leaves
Hissing through the cold heart of a dreary wood.
—I hear the voice!—woe! woe! unto the city—woe!
  woe! woe!

     [*He rushes away shrieking.*]

 1st Man. O base and wretched cowards! by the
  shrieks
Of a poor madman scar'd and terrified!
Thus they who take their conscience by the beard,

And laugh to scorn the voice that cannot lie,
At their own shadows start! now palsy-stricken
By the ravings of a drivelling idiot.
    1st Woman. See where heaven dawns on hell! Even
        in the path
Of that tormented demon, onward floats
An Angel! Mercy following Despair!
    2d Woman. Let us fall down and worship her.

[*Enter* MAGDALENE *dressed in white, with a Bible in her hand.*]

    1st Woman. It is the lovely Lady no one knows,
Who walks through lonesome places day and night,
Giving to the poor who have no earthly friend;
To the dying comfort—to the dead a grave!
I am a harden'd sinner—yet my heart
Softens at that smile, and when I hear her voice
I feel as in my days of innocence.
        [*They kneel down before her.*]
    Magd. Rise up my sisters and my brothers rise!
    Voice. How graciously she speaks unto the poor!
Angels have walk'd this earth—if thou art one,
And that voice tells thou art, whate'er its words,
Let us still kneel before thee!—sinful we!
And in our lives most desperately wicked;
Yet child of heav'n! believe us when we say
Religion hath not wholly left our hearts.

Scene III. THE CITY OF THE PLAGUE.

Magd. O piteous spectacle! by my very birth
I am a creature sinful as yourselves!
And if my life have freer been from guilt,
I owe the blessing of my innocence
To Him whose blood can change the hue of sin
Into the whiteness of thrice-driven snow.

  2d Woman. We are too wicked now to hope for pardon.

  Magd. Ye are not lost, but think that ye are so,
And therefore will not hope. Cheer up your souls!
Calmness will lead to hope, and hope to faith,
And faith unto that awful happiness
That walks unquaking through the shades of death,
Triumphant over nature's agony.

  2d Woman. Walk not away! speak to us yet awhile!

  Madg. Return unto your homes all ye that own
A home—a blessing even when desolate.
If young or old or sick be pining there,
Think on the comfort of the Comforter.
If all have perish'd, turn your eyes to Him
Who dwells in Zion, and you need not fear
The dreadful stillness of unlook'd for death.
I will pray with you; ne'er forget your prayers!
Even now you felt how sweet it was to bless
Me a poor sinful creature, since you think
That nature fram'd me kind and pitiful.
Pray unto Him who lov'd you on the cross!
Evening and morn and noon-day worship Him,

And what although your homes be desolate !
Your hearts will sing for joy—even as the lark
'Mid evening sunshine hymning up the sky,
Forgetful that since morn the spoiler's hand
Had torn her low-built nest.

 2d Woman.   O that the Plague
Would strike me dead before thou disappear—
For when thy heavenly face hath pass'd away,
What shall protect me from the ghastly looks,
The broken voice of guilt and agony ?

 Madg. Promise to pass this night in prayer.
 Several voices.   We promise.
 1st Man. She is indeed most beautiful ! O misery
To think that heaven is but a dream of fools !
Why gaze I on her thus, as if I felt her
To be immortal ! Something touch'd my soul
In that sad voice which earth can ne'er explain,
Something quite alien to our troubled being,
That carried on my soul into the calm
Of that eternal ocean !—Can it be ?
Can a smile—a word—destroy an atheist's creed ?
—Ha ! this is mockery !

 2d Woman.   See how she waves
Her snow-white hand from which a blessing falls
On all the crowded street ! How silently
The starry midnight passes o'er our heads !
How gladsome the pure moonlight ! Oh ! that angel
Hath by her beauty and her innocence

Won the great God of mercy to look down
On the children of despair. We part in peace!

SCENE IV.

FRANKFORT *sitting beside the bodies of his mother and little brother.—The* PRIEST *and* WILMOT *standing at some distance.*

 Frankfort. Thou need'st not look with such sad eyes
  on me.
Beloved old man! on that countenance
I now have gaz'd so long, that its deep calm
Hath sunk into my heart.
 Priest.   The comforter
Hath come to thee in solitude.
 Frank.   When left
With this still image I confess my voice
Called upon her loud and franticly
To start up into life. Even then a smile
Came o'er her face, a sweet upbraiding smile
That silently reprov'd my senseless grief.
O look upon her face! eternity
Is shadow'd there! a pure immortal calm
Whose presence makes the tumult of this world
Pass like a fleeting breeze, and through the soul
Breathes the still ether of a loftier climate!
 Priest. Many sweet faces have I seen in death,
But never one like this. Death beautifies

Even the stern face of guilt, and I have seen
The troubled countenance of a sinful man
Breath'd over, soon as life had pass'd away,
With a soft delicate shade,—as from the wing
Of Innocence returning to shed tears
Over the being she had lov'd in youth.
But here lies perfect beauty! her meek face
Free as that child's from any touch of sin,
Yet shining with that loftier sanctity
That holds communion with the promis'd heavens.

 Frank. (*To* Wilmot.) Kind friend! thou weep'st!
  Such tears will not disturb
Her sleep! see where they trickle silently
Down that unmoving cheek that feels them not,
As if they flowed from eyes that may not weep.

 Wil. My friend! may I kneel down and kiss her
  cheek.

 Frank. Start not at feeling that fair face so cold!
I often said that I would bring my friend
To see my mother.—Lo! I have fulfill'd
My promise! There she lies!

 Wil.   As I touch'd her lips
Methought her dead face smil'd a blessing on me!

 Frank. Take thou this ringlet of her auburn hair:
'Tis a sweet auburn, mingled though it be
With the soft silvery-grey! and be it blended
With these thick-clustering curls of undim'd joy,
In beauty parted from the radiant head

Of this delightful child—and for my sake
Keep them for ever!
  Priest.   If deserv'd by love
Part of these holy relics should be mine.
  Frank. Aye! aye!—Now may I ask whose pious care
Hath plac'd these death-flowers here! Methinks I read
In the fair disposition of these flowers
The delicate language of a female hand,
Not unforgetful of the skill that cheer'd
Its hours of happier task, even in the sad
Graceful adornment of the dead! One hand,
One hand alone on all the earth was worthy
To place these flowers—but it is far away!
  Priest. What if that hand it were?
  Frank.   Nay! mock me not.
Haply thou heardest not my words aright.
  Priest. One hand alone thou rightly said'st was worthy
To fix that wreath. The fingers of that hand
Stirr'd not the braided hair that they did touch,
Nor mov'd one fold upon the funeral sheet,
So that the flowers they shed seem'd dropping there
In a dewy shower from heaven! Thy Magdalene
It was indeed whose fingers dress'd the dead.
  Frank. Magdalene! and in the midst of this fell
   Plague!
Mine is a most mysterious destiny.
—O spirit of my mother! pardon me
Though with thy dead body lying in my sight

My soul with pangs returns unto the living,
If Magdalene indeed be with the living!—
That smile hath life in it. O blest old man,
Thou art indeed the servant of the Lord!

Priest. She lives! and even now is on her way
To attend thy mother's funeral!

Frank. Speak—speak—

Priest. She is an orphan.

Frank. O my heart is dry!
Were Magdalene's self a corpse I could not weep.

Priest. I need not tell at length the mournful tale.
Three happy weeks with their delighted daughter
They walk'd the city—and the day was fix'd
For their return unto their native mountains.
But the Plague came······

Frank. (*Passionately.*) They surely were not thrown
In the face of pity weeping all in vain,
Together thrown into that ghastly pit······

Priest. 'Twas easy then to find a place of rest
In consecrated ground, and they were buried,
The very day they died, in a quiet spot
Even not without its beauty, at the foot
Of a small tree that Nature's self had planted,
In a city church-yard standing quite alone.

Frank. And where was Magdalene on the burial-day?

Priest. I must not speak to thee of that one day!
But it is past and gone, and Magdalene
Is living. This is all I dare to utter.

There is an air that memory may not breathe,
And black oblivion hath her sacred ground
Guarded for aye by woe and misery.

Frank. Buried in a city 'mid a crowd of tombs!
Those floating locks blench'd by the ocean storms
Through many a perilous midnight—and that head
On which the snows of age were gently falling
Through the hush'd air of peace—both in the earth!
—Spoke they not of a burial-place far off?

Priest. They did—but with a smile.

Frank. It matters not.
—There is a little church-yard on the side
Of a low hill, that hangs o'er Rydal-lake,
Behind the house where Magdalene was born.
Most beautiful it is; a vernal glade
Enclos'd with wooded rocks! where a few graves
Lie shelter'd, sleeping in eternal calm.
Go thither when you will, and that green spot
Is bright with sunshine. There they hop'd to lie!
And there they often spoke to Magdalene
Of their own dying day. For death put on
The countenance of an angel in the place
Which he had sanctified. I see the spot
Which they had chosen for their sleep—but far,
O far away from that sweet sanctuary
They rest, and all its depth of sunny calm.
Methinks my Magdalene never dare return
To her native cottage.

Priest. No! she only smil'd
When I implor'd her to forsake the city;
Then said she would not leave her parents' bones.
Fain had she each day visited your mother,
But fear'd to bring infection——

Frank. O my mother!
Forgive me heaven! I had not sure forgotten
That I am listening to thee by her coffin!
My Magdalene's care was vain—she came at last
As these sad death-flowers tell.

Priest. Not in some spot
Apart from death, in deathlike loneliness
Doth Magdalene dwell. Throughout the livelong day,
And many a livelong night, for these three months
Hath she been ministering at the dying bed
From which, with an unnatural cowardice,
Affection, ardent in the times of joy,
Had fled,—perhaps to stumble o'er the grave.
—What! though thy Magdalene heretofore had known
Only the name of sorrow, living far
Within the heart of peace, with birds and flocks,
The flowers of the earth, and the high stars of heaven
Companions of her love and innocence;
Yet she who in that region of delight,
Slumber'd in the sunshine, or the shelter'd shade,
Rose with the rising storm, and like an angel
With hair unruffled in its radiance, stood
Beside the couch of tossing agony!

Scene IV.   THE CITY OF THE PLAGUE.   107

As undisturb'd as on some vernal day
Walking alone through mountain-solitude,
To bring home in her arms a new-yean'd lamb
Too feeble for the snow!
 Frank.   I wonder not!
Its beauty was most touching, and I loved
The bright and smiling surface of her soul;
But I have gazed with adoration
Upon its awful depths profoundly calm,
Seen far down shadowing the sweet face of heaven.
 Priest. Many think she bears a charm against the
  Plague;
And they are not deceiv'd. A charm she hath,
But hidden not in ring or amulet,
Sleeping in the quiet of her sinless soul.
Some think she is a spirit—many look
With tears of sorrow on a mortal creature
Whom death may steal away—but all agree
That a thing so piteous, kind, and beautiful,
Did never walk before upon this earth.
  [*The door opens, and* MAGDALENE *enters.*]
 Priest. Behold the blessed one of whom we speak!
 *Magdalene. (seeing Frankfort and Wilmot kneeling
  with their faces on the bed.)*
Haply some sorrowing friends unknown to me!
 Frank. (rising.) Magdalene! my holy Magdalene!
 Magd. [*throwing herself down beside him.*]
Hush! hush! my Frankfort! thus I fold one arm

Round thy blest neck, and with the other thus
I touch the silent dead!

Frank.   O Magdalene!
'Tis a wild night of bliss and misery.

Magd. We both are orphans.

Frank.   Hush! I know it all.—
An angel's arms are round me—No! a mortal's—
A mortal thing sublimed and beautified
By woes that would have broken many a heart.
In thy embrace what do I care for death!
In ev'ry breathing of thy holy bosom
I feel contentment, faith, and piety;
Nor can the shadow of this passing world
Breathed o'er thy face of perishable beauty
Bedim thy holy spirit—it is bright,
Nor seems to heed that gushing flood of tears.

Priest to Wilmot. Let us retire. The hour is draw-
      ing near,
Fixed for the funeral.

Wilmot.   Heaven in mercy sent
That angel with her dewy voice, and eyes
More dewy still, to stand beside the grave,
And shew my friend how beautiful in heaven
His mother now must be! That silent smile
To resignation might convert despair!
                     [*Priest and Wilmot retire.*]

SCENE V.

*A church-yard—midnight—a clear moon and serene sky—
a new dug grave close to the church-wall, on which are
leaning the Sexton and his assistant.*

Sexton. 'Tis a decent job enough; for a beginner
You handle your spade in no unpromising way,
And when our church-yard business revives,
(Confound that pit with its great ugly mouth—
'Tis the ruin of the trade)—you'll make my boy
A very pretty grave-digger. But hark-ye!
When standing good five feet below the sod,
Keep thine eyes open, and do'nt fling the gravel
Into my face, thou screech-owl. Stretch thyself
Up boldly like the son of a grave-digger,
And form the bank above thee neat and trim.
I wish to have some credit in my graves;
And even although the kinsfolk be poor judges,
And mind these things but little, I have an eye,
A grave-digger's eye, that loves to a nicety
To see a trench drawn for its own dear sake.
—Why art thou shivering there thou Aspen-leaf?

Boy. I never liked to walk through a church-yard.
And now at the very dead hour o' the night,
This standing overhead within a grave
Hath made me colder than an icicle,—
Aye, numb as any grave-stone of them all.

I would not care to dig a grave in a field
Out in the country, and by good day-light;
But to keep poking in a deep black-hole,
In the middle of a pavement of grave-stones,
With such a ghostlike moon above one's head,
And flinging out, instead of good plain pebbles,
Still yellow-grinning and worm-eaten skulls!
—'Tis shocking work.

Sexton. Fie! you disgrace your trade
You jackanapes! an ancient noble trade.
I'll get some bungler of a village-sexton,
Some bell-ringer well vers'd in psalmody
To bury thee like a dog, and lay thy coffin
With the wrong end to the headstone. Out on thee!

Boy. I think old man! with both feet in the grave
As one may say......

Sexton. Ho! ho! advice thou parrot!
With both feet in the grave! I will be singing
Over my work for many a year to come,
When thou, and chicken-hearted birds like thee,
Will all be caged. Death loves a grave-digger,
And would not hurt a hair upon his head.
As for the Plague he is afraid of us—
With a mattock and a shovel o'er my shoulder
He looks at me, and passes to such game
As thou, and smooth-fac'd maidens like to thee.

Boy. Didst ever see the lady and her child
Whose grave we have been digging—for if so,

Scene V.   THE CITY OF THE PLAGUE.   111

And yet hast felt no pity at thy work,
Thou would'st not scruple for a yellow King Charles
To bury a Christian lying in a trance.

Sexton. Six years ago, I buried her good husband,
As proper brave a man as e'er was laid
Under the turf. I have known the family
Three generations, and I loved them all.
But where's the use of whimpering like a child
That never saw a grave? Yet by my spade,
I think if I had any tears to shed
I would waste them all upon this very mould!
For a sweeter lady never walk'd to church
Nor stepp'd across a grave-stone. She is in heaven!
And he who thinks so well may dig her grave,
As merrily as a gard'ner in the spring.

Boy. See! yonder two men standing with drawn
swords!
We shall be murder'd.

Sexton.   Murder'd! that's a trifle.
But robb'd of all our money. Hold it fast
If you know where to find it—grave-diggers
Still carry gold about them at their work.
They'll murder, rob, and bury us in a twinkling.

   [*The Sexton and Boy stand silent within the shadow
       of the Church-wall, and* WALSINGHAM *and* FITZ-
       GERALD *approach.*]

Fitz. This place is fitter for our present purpose
Than that we fix'd before. Here is a grave

Just ready for thy body Walsingham!
Thou mayest have warmer lodgings for the night
At the price of one small word—" forgiveness."
  Walsingham. Methinks such high-toned pride but ill
    becomes
A scene like this. What! ask forgiveness
Of such a thing as thou—while the Great God
Beholds us standing here with murd'rous thoughts
Upon the dark brink of eternity.
Think what thou art, and what thou soon mayest be.
  Fitz. Fool! villain! liar! thus do I retort
Thy insupportable words. Thine is the pride—
The harden'd scorn is thine. But the hour is past,
In which I might have pardon'd thee—and now
Look at this rapier, and prepare to die.
  Wal. I am no coward. Yea! I wish to die—
But in the shadow of the house of God,
I must not be a murderer.
  Fitz.   House of God!
Right pious words! but they will not avail thee!
I think the Plague might well have scared such dreams,
Best cherish'd in the nursery, or by women
Whose faint hearts lean when sinking on religion.
God cares, forsooth, for us his worshippers!
Yet though we perish thousands in one night,
And like the brutes are buried, still we call him
Lord—Priest and Father, and still hope to rise
Even from the crowded pit where we lie smother'd

Like bees in brimstone,—to rise beautiful,
And soar to God's throne, spirits glorified!
O bitter mockery! Look into that pit
With all its dread corruption steaming up
To heaven, like an unheeded sacrifice,
And then dare talk of immortality.

   Sexton (discovering himself.)
I crave your pardon—but I did not dig
That grave for you, much-honour'd gentlemen.
It is bespoken, and the worthy owner
In half an hour will come to take possession.
I have heard of people fighting for small cause
Or none—but cutting throats in a church-yard
Is something new, and 'tis an ugly practice.

   Fitz. (rushing on Walsingham.)
                       Here's at thy heart!
   [*He receives Walsingham's sword in his heart, and
     falls, exclaiming,*]
                  O Christ! stone-dead! stone-dead!
   Sexton. Killing no murder—'twas in self-defence.
You've a quick eye, good Sir! or he had pink'd you.
These swords are ugly and unhandy things,
I never liked them.

   Wal.   Now I am a murderer!
That hideous name befits me! I have sent him
In all the blindness of his atheist heart
To his dread audit! Pho! his blood will redden
Upon my hands for ever. Wretch that I am!

Sexton. I hear them coming.

Wal. Whom dost thou hear coming?

Sexton. Listen! and hear the holy sound of psalms.

[*The funeral approaches the grave where* WALSINGHAM *is sitting near the dead body,—*MAGDALENE, ISABEL, PRIEST, FRANKFORT, *and* WILMOT.]

Priest. What shocking sight is this? O Walsingham,
My much-beloved and much-erring boy!
I fear that thou hast done a deed of sin,
For which remorse will haunt thee all thy days.

Wal. I hear thy voice, but dare not lift my eyes
Up to thy solemn countenance. I could bear
Thy anger, but the pity of the righteous
Speaks to the little virtue that is left
In my distracted soul, and when I hear it,
O that in dumb deaf darkness I could lie!

Frank. We two are brothers in calamity.

Wal. Frankfort? O now I know who fills that coffin.
Behold how with these blood-bedabbled hands
I tremble in the presence of her corpse.
Look here—look here—upon this stiffening body!
Its face convuls'd, cries out " a murderer!"

[*He flings himself down.*]

Sexton. Manslaughter at the worst. There was no murder.

Frank. He heeds us not—lost in the agony

Of his remorse. A more compassionate spirit—
One more averse to the shedding of man's blood,
Yet of his own more prodigal, never graced
The name of seaman.

  Priest.   Shall we drop the coffin
Into the grave? The hour has come at last!
Art thou prepar'd to hear the funeral service?
Or wilt thou go behind that tomb and wait——

  Wal. The funeral service is most beautiful,
And I can listen to it with the tears
Of a resigned sorrow. I remember
The day before I bade a last farewell
To her who is in heaven—we did partake
Together of the body of our Lord.
As we were walking homewards from the church,
With eyes where a sublime devotion smil'd
My mother looked at me, and gently whisper'd,
" Whate'er may be thy doom I feel resign'd;
" And if *I am not* when my son returns,
" Recall to mind this blessed sacrament,
" And think of me with Christ."

  Magd.   Lean on my heart,
For now the trial comes.

             (*The coffin descends into the grave.*)

  Frank.   Fling, fling the earth
Less rudely on her coffin! Magdalene!
See how it disappears! O final close,

To sunny years of joy and happiness!
All perish'd in that dull and hideous sound!

Magd. No mortal ever led a happier life.
Her husband died and she was sorrowful,—
But misery ne'er disturb'd her soul serene,
That like a place of worship aye was husht
By day and night,—or with the voice of hymns
Singing most sweetly to the ear of heaven.

Frank. I wonder not so much that she hath died,
As that a soul so perfect should have liv'd
So long in this sad world.—My little William,
Buried in all thy beauty—fare thee well!
Thank God! I never said an unkind word
To the sweet infant! Tears were in his eyes,
When last I went to sea—and when I said,
That I would bring him home the loveliest shells,
He smil'd and wept. His face is smiling now
Far, far down in the darkness of the grave.

[*They all kneel down around the grave.*]

END OF THE SECOND ACT.

THE
CITY OF THE PLAGUE.

ACT III.

SCENE I.

The PRIEST *and* WILMOT *walking in a square of the City.—Evening after the funeral of* FRANKFORT'S *mother.*

Wil. How sweetly have I felt the evening-calm
Come o'er the tumult of the busy day
In a great city! when the silent stars
Stole out so gladsome through the dark-blue heavens,
All undisturb'd by any restless noise
Sent from the domes and spires that lay beneath
Hush'd as the clouds of night.
    Priest.   Even now 'tis so.
Did'st thou e'er see a more resplendent moon?
A sky more cloudless—thicker set with stars?
    Wil. The night is silent—silent was the day.
But now methinks that sky's magnificence

Darkeneth the desolation on the earth!
Even such the silence of a beautiful sea
Rolling o'er a thousand wrecks.
 Priest.   Let us sit down
Upon this seat beneath its sheltering trees;
And if my soul can face the fearful things
Which it has seen and suffer'd, thou shalt hear
How a whole city perish'd—a whole city!
For, walking on the shore, we rightly call
The ocean calm, though distant waves be breaking
With melancholy dash against the rocks.
 Wil. Fit place it is for such wild colloquy!
These empty houses and that half-built spire
Standing with all its idle scaffolding ······
 Priest. I see a thousand sights thou can'st not see,
Glimmering around me—confused sights of woe
Mingling in the train of joy and happiness.
Sweet lovely children all around my feet
Are sporting—for this wide square was the play-ground
Where the bright families of prosperous men
Walk'd in the sunshine with their fairy dresses,
Laughing 'mid the flowers!—O many a slow-pac'd hearse
I see—and little coffins borne along
Beneath some solitary mourner's arm.
Mix'd are these images of life and death!
For while I muse upon the silent face
Of one dead infant, crowds of living spirits

Come singing by—and though I see a coffin,
They see it not, but glide with sunny feet
O'er the black pall, then disappear for ever.
   Wil. Came it on a sudden?
   Priest.   Like a thunder-peal
One morn a rumour turn'd the city pale;
And the tongues of men wild-staring on each other
Utter'd with faultering voice one little word,
" The Plague !" Then many heard within their dreams
At dead of night a voice foreboding woe,
And rose up in their terror, and forsook
Homes in the haunted darkness of despair
No more endurable. As thunder quails
Th' inferior creatures of the air and earth,
So bowed the Plague at once all human souls,
And the brave man beside the natural coward
Walk'd trembling. On the restless multitude,
Thoughtlessly toiling through a busy life,
Nor hearing in the tumult of their souls
The ordinary language of decay,
A voice came down that made itself be heard,
And they started from delusion when the touch
Of Death's benumbing fingers suddenly
Swept off whole crowded streets into the grave.
Then rose a direful struggle with the Pest!
And all the ordinary forms of life
Mov'd onwards with the violence of despair.
Wide flew the crowded gates of theatres,

And a pale frightful audience, with their souls
Looking in perturbation through the glare
Of a convulsive laughter, sat and shouted
At obscene ribaldry and mirth profane.
There yet was heard parading through the streets
War-music, and the soldier's tossing plumes
Mov'd with their wonted pride.   O idle shew
Of these poor worthless instruments of death,
Themselves devoted! Childish mockery!
At which the Plague did scoff, who in one night
The trumpet silenc'd and the plumes laid low.
As yet the Sabbath-day—though truly fear
Rather than piety fill'd the house of God—
Receiv'd an outward homage.   On the street
Friends yet met friends, and dar'd to interchange
A cautious greeting—and firesides there were
Where still domestic happiness surviv'd
'Mid an unbroken family; while the soul,
In endless schemes to overcome the Plague,
In art, skill, zeal, in ruth and charity
Forgot its horrors, and oft seem'd to rise
More life-like 'mid the ravages of death.
But soon the noblest spirits disappear'd,
None could tell whither—and the city stood
Like a beleagur'd fortress that hath lost
The flower of its defenders.   Then the Plague
Storm'd, raging like a barbarous conqueror,
And hopeless to find mercy every one

Fell on his face, and all who rose again
Crouch'd to the earth in suppliant agony.

Wil. Father! how mournful every Sabbath-day
To miss some well-known faces! to behold
The congregation weekly thinn'd by death,
And empty seats with all their Bibles lying
Cover'd with dust.

Priest. Aye—even the house of God
Was open to the Plague. Amid their prayers
The kneelers sicken'd, and most deadly-pale
Rose up with sobs,—and beatings of the heart
That far off might be heard, a hideous knell
That ne'er ceas'd sounding till the wretches died.
Sometimes the silent congregation sat
Waiting for the priest, then stretch'd within his shroud.
Or when he came, he bore within his eyes
A trouble that disturb'd, and read the service
With the hollow voice of death.

Wil. Where was the king?
The nobles and the judges of the land?

Priest. They left the city. Whither—none inquir'd.
Who cares now for the empires of the earth,
Their peerage or their monarchs? Kingly ones
Sit unobserv'd upon their regal seats,
And the soul looks o'er ocean, earth and air,
Heedless to whom its fields or waves belong,
So that there were some overshadowing grove
Central amid a mighty continent,

Or sacred island in the healthful main
Where men might be transported in a thought
Far from the wild dominion of the Plague.
Now He is monarch here—nor mortal brow
Durst wear a crown within the fatal sweep
Of his long bony arm.

Wil.   He loves the silence
Of an unpeopled reign.

Priest.   Once at noon-day
Alone I stood upon a tower that rises
From the centre of the city. I look'd down
With awe upon that world of misery;
Nor for a while could say that I beheld
Aught save one wide gleam indistinctly flung
From that bewildering grandeur: Till at once
The objects all assum'd their natural form,
And grew into a City stretching round
On every side, far as the bounding sky.
Mine eyes first rested on the squares that lay
Without one moving figure, with fair trees
Lifting their tufted heads unto the light,
Sweet, sunny spots of rural imagery
That gave a beauty to magnificence.
Silent as nature's solitary glens
Slept the long streets—and mighty London seem'd,
With all its temples, domes, and palaces,
Like some sublime assemblage of tall cliffs
That bring down the deep stillness of the heavens

To shroud them in the desert. Groves of masts
Rose through the brightness of the sun-smote river,
But all their flags were struck, and every sail
Was lower'd. Many a distant land had felt
The sudden stoppage of that mighty heart.
Then thought I that the vain pursuits of man
Possess'd a semblance of sublimity,
Thus suddenly o'erthrown; and as I look'd
Down on the courts and markets, where the soul
Of this world's business once roar'd like the sea,
That sound within my memory strove in vain,
Yet with a mighty power, to break the silence
That like the shadow of a troubled sky
Or moveless cloud of thunder, lay beneath me,
The breathless calm of universal death.

Wil. I feel all fears for my own worthless self
Vanish at thy voice—but it grows tremulous—
I now will hear no more. I know not why
My soul thus longs to feast itself on terror—
Last night I saw enough. O that church-yard!
That madman's dance!

Priest. My voice is tremulous,
For I shall never see fourscore again.
But I can speak to thee about the Plague
That rages round us, with as calm a soul
As if a hundred years had pass'd away
Since yonder Pest-house heard the groans and shrieks
Of more than mortal agony.

Wil.   A Pest-house!
O dreadful habitation! I beheld it,
As if in silence standing tenantless.
List! list! what fearful cries! They will burst the walls,
And issue forth a ghost-like company
Into the frighten'd air. Now—now—'tis silent!
As if in that one shriek they all had perish'd.

Priest. Let not thy spirit penetrate its walls.
Our Saviour pities it.

Wil.   And who will go
Into such tomb-like building fill'd with horror?

Priest. Aye! 'tis a dreadful mansion standing there
So black! as if the very walls did know
The agony within. Yet hither come
The children of despair and poverty,
Who baring bosoms yellow with Plague-spots
Implore admittance, and with hollow voice
Do passionately vow their gratitude,
If suffer'd to lay down their rending heads
On the straw pallets—so that skilful men
May visit them, even when the wretches say
They have no hope. Poor souls! perhaps they die
In mitigated agony at last;
But when a ghost-like shadow enters there
It sees the sun no more.

Wil.   Didst thou e'er pray
Within that fearful tabernacle?

Priest.   Yes!

'Tis but two nights ago I thither went
To minister the sacrament. I heard
A hideous din before I reach'd the door—
And entering I beheld the ghastly patients
Walking tumultuously throughout the room,
Some seemingly in anger—all the rest
In mute despair. There lay th' attendants dead!
And thirst had come upon that pale-fac'd crew
Who gasp'd, and made wild motions with their hands,
When in their parch'd mouths prayers or curses died.
　Wil. It was most horrible.
　Priest.　　　　　　But I have witness'd
A sight more hideous still. The Plague broke out
Like a raging fire within the darksome heart
Of a huge mad-house; and one stormy night
As I was passing by its iron gates,
With loud crash they burst open, and a troop
Of beings all unconscious of this world,
Possess'd by their own fearful phantasies,
Did clank their chains unto the troubled moon
Fast rolling through the clouds. Away they went
Across the glimmering square! some hurriedly
As by a whirlwind driven, and others moving
Slow—step by step—with melancholy mien,
And faces pale in ideot-vacancy.
For days those wild-eyed visitors were seen
Shrieking—or sitting in a woeful silence,
With wither'd hands, and heaps of matted hair!

And they all died in ignorance of the Plague
That freed them from their cells.—

Wil.   Do none recover
Whom the Plague strikes?

Priest.   Not one in many thousands.
Yet two such wretches have I chanced to see,
And they are living still—far better dead!
For they have lost all memory of the past,
All feeling of the future. Their own names
They know not—nor that they are human beings.
Like images of stone there do they sit,
When all around is agony; or laugh,
As if their features only were convuls'd,
In the absence of all soul! Aye, long and loud
The laughter is of those stone-images,
Sitting unmov'd with their glaz'd steadfast eyes!
And none can tell why the poor wretches laugh
Who know not how to weep.

Wil.   How many children
Must have died in beauty and in innocence
This fatal summer!

Priest.   Many sweet flowers died!
Pure innocents! they mostly sank in peace.
Yet sometimes it was misery to hear them
Praying their parents to shut out the Plague;
Nor could they sleep alone within their beds,
In fear of that dread monster. Childhood lost
Its bounding gladsomeness—its fearless glee—

And infants of five summers walk'd about
With restless eyes, or by their parents' sides
Crouched shuddering, for they ever heard them speak-
    ing
Of death, or saw them weeping—no one smiled.
  Wil. Hath not the summer been most beautiful,
'Mid all this misery?
  Priest.   A sunny season!
What splendid days, what nights magnificent
Pass'd in majestic march above the City,
When all below was agony and death!
" O peaceful dwellers ! in yon silent stars,
" Burning so softly in their happiness!"
Our souls exclaimed,—" unknown inhabitants
" Of unknown worlds ! no misery reaches you,
" For bliss is one with immortality!"
The very river as it flowed along
Appear'd to come from some delightful land
Unknown unto the Plague, and hastening on
To join the healthful ocean, calmly smil'd,
A privileged pilgrim through the realms of death.
Yea! in the sore disturbance of men's souls
They envied the repose of lifeless things!
And the leafy trees that grac'd the city-squares,
Bright with the dews of morning, they seem'd blest!
On them alone th' untainted air of heaven
Shed beauty and delight—all round them died.
London alone, of all the world seem'd curst.

O happy spots in country—or in town!
'Mid savage wilds—or dark and noisome streets—
Cut off from human intercourse—or haunted
By vice and sorrow, penury and guilt,
Ye seem'd to all a blessed Paradise,
Whether on wings of rapture they would fly
Nor ever leave you more—for nature groans
" Where the Plague is not, there dwells happiness."

   Wil. Dreadful indeed, to think how months and
      months
Have pass'd and still are passing without hope.

   Priest. In church-yards, not in houses, it did seem
As if the people lived. They haunted there.
It was, you well may think, a woeful sight
In every burial-ground to see the grave-stones
Blacken'd o'er with persons, sitting night and day,
Bewailing their lost friends. But sadder still,
Ere long to see the self-same tombstones bare,
Telling how few at last were left to weep.
Sometimes I take my solitary stand
In one of those wide church-yards. Onwards pass
A multitude of faces recognised
Dimly, as beings vanish'd from this world:
Till as I gaze upon them, memory
Disowns the wild creation of my brain,
And the image of those countless myriads,
Some strange procession seems of unknown creatures
On some unknown occasion moving by,

And cloud-like disappearing from my soul,
A shifting pageant journeying endless on!
　Wil. And all immortal souls! sent from this world
As by a breath! like insects vanishing
On a sudden, when a breeze comes o'er the silence
Of a sultry summer-noon!—
　Priest.　　　　　　　What meets thine eyes?
　Wil. Lo! yonder Frankfort walking toward us.
Is there not something wild in his appearance?
I trust that all is well with Magdalene.
Alas! should she be dead!
　Priest.　　　　　'Tis for himself
I fear that we must weep.—That devious pace,
Now stopping on a sudden—and now hurried
As by a raging wind against the will......
I tremble to behold it—for the Pest
Oft dallies thus with its delirious victims.
And yet some agitation of the mind......
　　[*Wilmot goes up to Frankfort as he is passing by
　　　distractedly without noticing them.*]
　Wil. Companion—messmate—friend—best, dearest
　　friend,
Wilt thou not speak to us?
　Frank.　　　　　　Hoist out the barge—
My crew will pull her through the roaring surf.
I have a mother dying of the Plague····
　Wil. Sweet friend! look, look around! O misery!
His mind is overthrown.

Frank.   Say who art thou
That glarest so upon me with thine eyes?
Hadst thou a brother once?
  Wil.   My name is Wilmot.
  Frank. Wilmot? Methinks I know thee! Wilmot!
      Wilmot!
  Wil. I owe my life to thee.
  Frank.   O merciful God!
A roaring whirlwind hurries off my soul—
I surely feel these stones beneath my feet;
Houses are standing round me—yet even now,
If ever sailor trod upon a deck
I was on board the Thunderer. What dark building
Towers yonder like a cloud? Is it a mad-house?
No irons on my hands·····O chain me—chain me—
In mercy to one steadfast place of earth,
Nor drive me onwards like a heaving wave
Over the midnight sea.
  Priest.   Touch this grey head!
  Frank. Old man! thou hast a kind and gentle look—
—Then tell me this, and I will bless thee for it.
Did a fair maiden come on board to day,
Calling herself, with a low mournful voice,
Magdalene Lambert? Did she ask for me
With that low mournful voice, and hath she gone
Weeping away because she found me not?
Drest is she all in white, as Poets feign
The angel Innocence—and when she speaks····

Wilmot, I know thee now—hath something dreadful
Fallen on my head—or am I in a fever,
And raving here with a distemper'd brain?
 Priest. We are indeed thy friends! Look at this hair
Which I am wearing close unto my heart
For thy dead mother's sake. Behold how softly
The silver-lined auburn doth repose,
Amid the sunshine of sweet William's ringlets.
  [*Frankfort falls on his neck and weeps.*]
 Frank. Conduct me home—home—home—whate'er
  I say.
But look not so....O ye dim ghastly faces,
I know ye not....I am your prisoner....
Lead, lead me hence, and chain me in my cell.
 Priest to Wilmot. Let us conduct him home! prepare
  thy soul
For what this night may happen to thy friend.
For death is in his face.

SCENE II.

MAGDALENE *seen lying asleep on a couch—*ISABEL *and a*
 YOUNG GIRL *sitting beside her.*

 Isabel. Didst thou e'er see so beautiful a face?
Lo! how it smiles through sleep! Even in her dreams
Her soul is at some work of charity.
 Child. May I go softly up, and kiss her cheek?
O why is it so pale?

Isabel. 'Twas always so.

Child. I thought that paleness was a mark of grief.
My mother's face was always deadly pale,
But then she often wept—I know not why.
This Lady must be happy.

Isabel. She awakes.

Child. Perhaps that kiss disturb'd her.

Isabel (to Magdalene who awakes.) Magdalene!
Thou scarcely seem'st to recollect this child.
'Tis she who follow'd thee from that house of death:
Look here—her small hands have already learn'd
To serve her gracious mistress; and this table
With such refreshments as thy need requires
They spread—an orphan's gratitude has blest them.

Magd. Wilt thou go hundreds of long weary miles,
Carried thou know'st not where, along with me
And that kind girl? A sister of our own
In a far-distant land thou then wilt be,
And all day run about green sunny hills
With little snow-white lambs, while happy birds
Sing to thee from their nests among the broom.

Child. I would go with thee to a land of ice
And everlasting snow.

Magd. How prone to love
Is the pure sinless soul of infancy!

Child. My father—mother—brothers—sisters all—
Are dead! yet Lady! when I hear thee speak,
I must be happy in spite of all the tears

That gush into mine eyes. My mother stood
Close to my pillow last night in a dream,
And bade me weep no more, for that an angel
Had folded over me her heavenly wings.
I woke—and there wert thou! at my bedside
With these delightful smiles.

Magd.　　　　　O Isabel!
Of all the mournful—sad—affecting things
That sorrow meets with in a world of sorrow,
The saddest sure those smiles of happiness,
Those sudden starts of uncontrollable glee
That, like the promptings of a different nature,
Assail the heart of childhood 'mid its grief,
And turn its tears to rapture. Beauteous beings!
Hanging in the air 'twixt joy and misery!
Now like the troubled sea-birds wildly-wailing
Through the black squall;—and now upon the billows
Alighting softly with the gleams of light,
They float in beauty of a fearless calm.

　Isabel. Why so profound a sigh?
　Magd.　　　　　　　　A deadly pain
Even at that moment struck into my heart.
A sudden fear disturbs me—look on my face—
Seest thou aught wild and strange within my eyes?
Fear not to speak the truth.
　Isabel.　　　　　O nought I see
Within these eyes but a meek tender light
Softer than swimming tears—and on thy face

The same pale beauty lies by all belov'd
Even when thou wert a child—a breathing paleness
More touching than the cheeks so rosy-red
Of other children—nothing else see I.

Magd. O shame! I feel the tears upon my cheek,
I weep that I must die. O days and nights
Past on my knees beside the bed of death,
Have ye been all in vain! I shudder at death
Even as this child would do—most mournful weakness!

Child. I would not fear to die within your arms.

Magd. Bring me yon little mirror here—sweet child!
And as you come with it, look in and see
As fair a face as ever Innocence
Put on to gladden her own gazing soul!

[*The Child gives the looking-glass to Magdalene,
who after a single glance continues,*]

One look into that glass reveal'd my fate.
I wish not to deceive my Isabel.
I feel that I am dying.

Isabel. (falling on her knees.) Merciful God!
Let the cup of death pass from her holy lips.

Magd. One momentary pang when torn from earth!
I am resign'd.

Isabel. O last night's awful scene,
Hath overcome thy body and thy soul.
Both are disquieted—but both ere long
Will wake to peace.—Assist me Margaret,

Scene II.   THE CITY OF THE PLAGUE.   135

And we two soft and silent as a dream
Will lay her on that bed.   How feels my mistress?
                              [*They support her to bed.*]
   Magd. Too well am I acquainted with the Plague,
And all its fatal symptoms.   I beheld
The slumb'rous weight upon my eyes, the dim
Blue shade that never more must leave my cheeks—
My lips are touch'd by death—before the hour
Of earliest morning—the small midnight hour—
—O Heaven protect my faithful Isabel,
And waft her safe, as on an angel's wing,
To that sweet Lake which I must see no more!
   Isabel. This world at once is darken'd.
   Magd.   Frankfort! come,
Or thy sweet voice will all be lost on me!—
—Last night I dreamt of death and burial:
The Plague had stricken me in my troubled sleep!
Look here—death-tokens on my breast!
      [*Isabel rushes into her arms and kisses her bosom.*]
   Isabel.   These kisses
Will cure my agony!   O savage death!
May not the touch of that angelic bosom
Win o'er to pity thy relentless soul!
O Christ! that mortal blueness hath been spread
By the chill air of the grave!
   Magd.   Kiss—kiss me not.
   Isabel. Till death come from thy bosom—I will kiss
      thee.

Child. Lady! I hear a soft tap at the door.
Magd. Then open it my little fearful maid,
For none but friends come here.
    [*Enters the* OLD PRIEST.]
Priest.   What! all in tears!
Isabel. O Sir! look here!—look here!
Priest.   My holy child!
O ghost-like now thy more than mortal beauty!
Can'st thou not raise thy head?
Magd.   O pray for me.
Priest. Daughter! thy name is well-beloved in
  heaven.
There hath been something in thy destiny
Above our human nature, and thy soul
Conspicuous, like a never-setting star,
Hath shone o'er all the city—shedding joy
And consolation. There is need of thee
In this most wicked and afflicted world,
And therefore do I trust with holy awe
That death's dark shadow will pass over thee,
And thou in undimm'd beauty reappear!
—If so the will of God!
Magd.   Thou must pray for me,
While yet I hear and understand thy prayers.
Too well thou thinkest of me—I am weak
In all my being—weaker far than many
Who have died unprais'd—unhallow'd and unwept.
O sinful pride! and base hypocrisy!

Scene II.   THE CITY OF THE PLAGUE.   137

If in the deep prostration of my soul
I did not so confess. My earthly nature,
With eager visitings to all unknown,
Oft haunted me, when I was kneeling down
In prayer with others—holding up the head
From which all sense was parting. Oh! my pity
Was oft imperfect—almost insincere!
Yet God may in his boundless love accept
My feeble efforts. Faith at least is mine.
Oh! were that gone I should be poor indeed.

Priest. Daughter! in happier mood thou could'st not
   die.

Magd. O father! when I liv'd in happiness,
I drank the cup of joy, and often fail'd
To thank the hand that gave it. Years pass'd by,
And still I grew and flourish'd, like a flower
Unconscious of the sun that blesseth it.
But now the sadness of ingratitude
Disturbeth me, when I have need of comfort.

Priest. God is well satisfied with innocence.
The pure soul best doth prove its gratitude
By acquiescence to his will supreme,—
Calm thoughts and meek desires,—unsought-for bliss
Coming to youth from all the points of heaven,—
And above all by natural piety
That sees love, beauty, and delight on earth,
And on their wings mounts every happy man
Up to the gates of heaven. Thy joyful years

Are not forgotten by the Power that gave them,
And not one virtuous, momentary thought
E'er stirr'd thy heart, that is not register'd
In the book of mercy—therefore calm thy soul.

Magd. I cannot doubt the language of these eyes,
So solemn—saint-like!—O were Frankfort happy!
I now could follow death into the grave
As joyfully as in the month of May
A lamb glides after its soft-bleating mother
Into a sunny field of untrod dew.
Heaven will protect my Isabel! Thou too
My well-beloved friend of yesterday
Wilt have a gentle father. Dry thy tears—
Yet youth will dry them for thee. If my Frankfort—

[*She starts suddenly up in bed.*]

Take—take away these hands before thy face
And tell me in one word—" is he alive?"

Priest. He is alive—but his perturbed soul
Is tost and driven throughout a ghastly dream.

Magd. Is he alone—in his insanity?
O that the Plague would prey upon our bodies,
But leave the spirit free!

Priest.   Wilmot is with him.

Magd. Eternal bliss be with that fearless friend!

Priest. It may not be the Plague.

Magd.   It is the Plague.
I know it is the Plague—and he will die.

Isabel. O lady! rise not up.

[MAGDALENE *rises from bed and stands in the midst of them.*]

Magd. What! remain here?
In what I say I must not be oppos'd.
You love me—therefore in your love be silent.
I go to Frankfort—I shall not fall down
In the street before I reach him. I feel strong,
And could walk many miles. Come Isabel.
Let me kiss the book of God before I go.—
Farewell my little room! Thou art indeed
A calm and peaceful cell—and I have past
Many still hours of awful happiness
Within thy lonely twilight. Now farewell!
I leave thee for a lodging calmer yet.

SCENE III.

FRANKFORT *lying on a bed in the house of his deceased mother.*—WILMOT *watching beside him.*

Frank. Go upon deck and tell me if thou seest
The signal flying for close line of battle.
Does our good vessel lead the van to-day?
Or will those tame and cautious Hollanders
Still keep a lee-shore on their skulking bows?

Wil. Look on me Frankfort—this is all a dream.

Frank. No time for jesting. Tell the old lieutenant
That a braver seaman never trod the deck,

But that I fight my ship myself to-day,
She is his when I am killed.
   Wil.   Look at this bed—
These curtains pictur'd o'er with little birds
Sporting in a grove of spring. Thy cabin, Frankfort,
Hath no such peaceful garniture. Look here,
We have no windows like to these at sea.
Frankfort thou art a right good seaman still,
And in thy raving fits must needs be fighting
With these poor Dutchmen.—Prithee let them rest
In their flat-bottom'd vessels for one day.
—Ha! thou art smiling!
   Frank.   Yes! I well may smile
At my poor wandering soul. Wilmot! a ship
Doth on the ocean hold the raging winds
At her command—queen-like, as doth become her.
But I am driven along a glimmering sea,
And know not how to bear up 'gainst the storm.
   Wil. Thank God you recognise your friend at last.
   Frank. I know thee now—but whether, the next moment,
Thy face may seem to me what now I think it,
God only knows. It is a dreadful state,
When, like a horse by lightning scar'd to madness,
One's soul flies with him wheresoe'er it will,
And still one feels that he is hurried on
But cannot stop—in terror hurried on—
Away—away—away—a frightful race!

Wil. Thou may'st remember what vagaries I
Once fell into, when that fierce tropic sun
Did smite my brain with fever. Then, heaven bless me!
I was far more pacific in my dreams,
And fancied all the world in love with me.

 Frank. What fool hath brought our vessel to an anchor?
Order the master down—by heaven the fleet
Will laugh us all to scorn. Hark, a broadside!
We are a long league in the admiral's wake
While he is closing with the enemy.
Hoist every inch of canvas—I will soon
Recover my lee-way.

 [*He leaps out of bed with great violence, and falls senseless on the floor. After a long fainting-fit he exclaims,*]

    Where am I Wilmot?—
Where art thou my pure spirit—where is Magdalene?

 Wil. She and the old Priest will be here anon.

 Frank. Is this a stormy night?

 Wil.   A perfect calm.

 Frank. The noise of thunder and tempestuous waves
Is raging in my soul.

 Wil.   'Tis all a dream.

 Frank. O hold me—hold me fast—keep, keep me here.
I am on board a ship, and she is sinking
Down to the very bottom of the sea.

She bounds up from the abyss—and o'er the billows
Rolls manageless—and now—now water-logg'd
Is settling—settling—till she sink like lead
Never to rise again! Hush—hush my crew!
In shipwreck fearless as in battle—hush!
Let us sink in silence to eternity.

Wil. On good dry land are we my boy! at last.
Though yet the rolling of our gallant ship
Is loth to leave our brains. Smile to me messmate.

Frank. Have we been travelling o'er foreign lands
And met adventures perilous and wild?
Thou seem'st to look on me with asking eyes!
Listen, and I will tell a fearful story:
But interrupt me not—for like a flood
That hath been all night raging 'mid the mountains
My soul descends from its wild solitude,
And must sweep on till all its troubled thoughts
Have from their headlong fury found repose.
Thou wilt not interrupt me?

Wil. No! sweet friend!

Frank. It seemeth many many years ago
Since I remember aught about myself,
Nor can I tell why I am lying here.
Before I fell into this dream, I saw
A most magnificent and princely square
Of some great city. Sure it was not London?
No—no—the form and colour of those clouds
So grim and dismal never horrified

The beautiful skies of England, nor such thunder
Ever so growl'd throughout my native clime.
It was the capital city of a kingdom
Lying unknown amid unvoyaged seas,
Where towers and temples of an eastern structure
With airy pomp bewilder'd all my soul.
When gazing on them I was struck at once
With blindness and decay of memory,
And a heart-sickness almost like to death.
A deep remorse for some unacted crime
Fell on me. There, in dizziness I stood,
Contrite in conscious innocence—repentant
Of some impossible nameless wickedness
That bore a dread relation unto me.
A ghastly old man—and a noble youth
Yet with fierce eyes that smil'd with cruelty,
Came up to me all lost in wonderment
What spots of blood might mean beneath my feet
All over a bed of flowers. The old man cried,
" Where is thy mother impious parricide !
" Ha ! thou hast buried her beneath these flowers."
The young man laugh'd and kick'd the flowers aside,
And there indeed my murder'd mother lay
With her face up to heaven ! imploring mercy
For her unnatural son. Then the old man
Touch'd my cold shoulder with his icy fingers,
And direful pains assail'd me suddenly—
Burnings and shiverings—flashings from my eyes—

And dizzy blindness whirling round my soul—
And arrowy sharpness tingling through my bones—
Until I wept in utter agony.
And all the while I saw my mother's corpse
Lying in peace before her frantic son,
And knew that I in wrath had murder'd her.
More dreadful was my doom than if my hand
Indeed had ta'en her life—for sure in sleep
The soul hath a capacity of horror
Unknown to waking hours. No fetter'd wretch,
Dragg'd on a sledge to execution,
E'er felt such horrid pangs as then stirr'd up
My spirit with remorseful agony.
O Wilmot! Wilmot! lead me to my mother—
That I with yearning soul may pour my kisses
O'er the dear frame I murder'd in my sleep.

Wil. Yesterday morning in this very bed
Your mother died a calm and peaceful death,
Blessing her son for all his piety.

Frank. O lying Fiend! Thou art the very youth
That shook the bloody flowers before my face,
And from the land of dreams hast follow'd me
In ghostly persecution to the light
Of this our upper world! Say! where is he,
The grey-hair'd Fiend in holy vestments clad?
O Christ! so wild a likeness in his wrath
Of my best earthly friend!—Upon my knees
I cry to thee—I shriek unto thy soul—

Art, art thou Wilmot?—Let me see thine eyes—
Oh! they are fill'd with tears! my brother weeps!
And well he may—for such a wretch as I am
God ne'er before abandon'd to despair.

Wil. Thy soul will climb into the light at last,
Out of its haunted darkness—fear it not.

Frank. The Plague! the Plague! the Plague! did
    she not die
Of the Plague? who saw her buried? No one—no
    one.—
Drive off that madman from my mother's grave,
And let that angel all array'd in light
Look down with her sunlike face into the pit,
Her smile will make it heaven. O Magdalene!
Thy spirit comes down from its rest on high
To glorify my mother's funeral.
Yes! What on earth we love and call it Pity,
In heaven we worship by a holier name,
Mercy! The seraph whom our Saviour loves.

Wil. She is alive. No tears need fall for him
Who, waking from a dream so steep'd in horror,
Hath such an one to bless him when he wakes.
Thy Magdalene lives.

Frank.   O heartless mockery!
Why camest thou here to talk of Magdalene?
Thou art leagued with all the world to murder me,
With that sweet name too beauteous to be borne.
I know that she is dead, and am resign'd.

K

But let her name die too—its syllables
Flame on my brain in letters form'd of fire,
A burning name, all, all that now remains.
  Wil. O I would die, so that my friend had peace.
  Frank. O Wilmot! Pity him the Plague hath
      stricken!
He knows not what he says. O pity me!
For I have undergone such mortal pains!
Whether in dreams or in a waking hell
I know not—but my soul hath suffer'd them—
And they have left me powerless as a sail
Hanging in the breathless calm. But list! I hear
Soft footsteps pattering all around my head—
Are they living feet?
  Wil.   Behold thy Magdalene.
[*Enter* MAGDALENE, PRIEST, ISABEL, *and* CHILD.]
  Frank. I see a groupe of faces known in youth—
All but the face of that delightful child—
And she admitted to such company
Must be what she appears—unknown to sin.
    [*Magdalene kneels down by the bedside and looks
      on Frankfort.*]
  Magd. Say that thou know'st me, and I shall die
      happy.
  Frank. Magdalene! for I will call thee by that name!
Thou art so beautiful!
  Magd.   Enough—enough!
  Frank. O Magdalene! why I am lying here,

And why so many melancholy faces
Are looking all at me, and none but me,
I now must never know. I see the tears
Which all around do shed are meant for me;
But none will tell me why they thus should weep.
Has some disgrace befallen me? One word,
One little word from thee will make all plain—
For oh! a soul with such a heavenly face,
Must live but in relieving misery!

 Magd. Disgrace and Frankfort's name are far asun-
  der,
As bliss from bale. O press my hand, sweet friend!
Its living touch may wake thee from thy dream
Of unsubstantial horrors. Magdalene
Hath come to die with thee—even in thy arms!

 Frank. O music well known to my rending brain—
It breathes the feeling of reality
O'er the dim world that hath perplex'd my soul.
All, all again is clear—I know myself—
Magdalene and Wilmot—Isabel and thee,
Beloved old man!—what may be the name
Of this small creature?

 Child.   Margaret Rivington.

 Frank. God bless thy sweet simplicity.

 Magd.   Thy face
Is all at once spread over with a calm
More beautiful than sleep, or mirth, or joy!
I am no more disconsolate. We shall die

Like two glad waves, that, meeting on the sea
In moonlight and in music, melt away
Quietly 'mid the quiet wilderness!

Frank. Sweet image to a sailor!—How my soul
Enjoys this quiet after its despair!
O might I lie for ever on the bed
Of sickness—so that such dear comforters
Might sit beside me! singing holy airs,
Or talking to each other, or to me,
Even to the very moment of my death.
The sweetest voice among so many sweet
My Magdalene's! and I the happy cause
Of all such tender looks and melting tones.

Magd. Frankfort hast thou look'd upon thy Magdalene's face?

Frank. (*Starting up.*) O God! remove that colour from her cheek—
That woeful glimmer of mortality!
Who brought thee hither from thy distant room?

Magd. On foot I came between two loving friends.
I felt not wearied then—but now I feel
That I can walk no more. Let me lie down
And die, as we two will be buried
Close to each other's side.

Frank. O cruel friends
To let thee walk so far with that pale face,
Weak as thou art to see a dying wretch
Like me!

[*They raise up* Magdalene, *and lay her on the bed beside* Frankfort.]

Magd. I hope thou feel'st no cruel pain?

Frank. Thy soft white spotless bosom, like the plumes
Of some compassionate angel, meets my heart!
And all therein is quiet as the snow
At breathless midnight.

Magd. No noise in thy brain?

Frank. A sweet mild voice is echoing far away
In the remotest regions of my soul.
'Tis clearer now—and now again it dies,
And leaves a silence smooth as any sea,
When all the stars of heaven are on its breast.

Magd. We go to sleep, and shall awake with God.

Frank. Sing me one verse of a hymn before I die.
Any of those hymns you sang long, long ago
On Sabbath evenings! Sob not so my Magdalene.

Magd. (*sings.*)

    Of Souls I see a glorious shew
      Beyond life's roaring flood!
    With raiment spotless as the snow,
      Wash'd white in Jesus' blood.

    His gentle hand their couch hath spread
      By many a living stream—
    No sigh is drawn—no tear is shed—
      One bright—eternal dream!

Frank. I cannot see thee—but I hear thy voice
Breathing assurance of the world to come.

I feel that I am dying—sinking down
As through soft-yielding waters murmuring round me,
Noiseless as air, and almost to be breathed.
It is the calm before the approach of death.
Kiss—kiss me Magdalene! I am sinking down—
Wilmot farewell—old man—kind Isabel—
Kiss—kiss me! ....

   Wil. to Priest. Death was in that long-drawn sigh.
   Priest. Our friend is gone.
   Magd. Yes! I have kiss'd his lips
And they are breathless. Let me lay my head
On thy unbeating bosom. O sweet hair
In stillness shadowing that delightful face
Where anger never came!—I see a smile
No living thing may borrow from the dead!
   Priest. She is composed.
   Magd. Yes father! I am blest.
This were a sight on which despair might look
With stony eyes and groan herself to madness.
But I am dying—therefore o'er the dead
Weep only tears of joy.
   Isabel. But o'er the living!
Oh!
   Magd. A drowsiness falls on me. Isabel
Let me sleep in Frankfort's arms. I shall awake
Refresh'd and happy in th' approach of death,
And whisper to thy ear my farewell words.
   Priest. She falls asleep! in that most death-like trance

Let us bear Frankfort's body to the grave !
—She may recover ! See her breath just moves
The ringlets on his cheek !—How lovingly
In her last sleep these white and gentle hands
Lie on his neck and breast !—Her soul is parting !
Had ever lovers such a death as this?
Let us all kneel and breathe our silent prayers !

SCENE IV.

A church-yard—midnight—a crowd of people assembled round the mouth of a huge pit dug for the interment of the dead.

   1st Man. Keep back my friends—so that each man may have
A fair view of the pit :—We all stand here
Upon a footing of equality,
And the less we crowd upon each other thus,
The better shall we see the spectacle.

   2d Man. What think ye ? Why the villain at the gate
Would have admittance-money, and stretched forth
His long lean shrivell'd fingers in my face,
Half-beggar and half-robber. Lying knave !
Who said he had not drawn a sous to-night :
For in his other palm I saw the edge
Of silver monies smiling daintily.
So I push'd the hoary swindler to the wall,
And, as he dropp'd the coin, I saw no harm

In picking up some stragglers for myself.
I wonder where will imposition end
Thus rife within the dwellings of the dead!

3d Man. This pit is not so wide by one good half
As that in Moorfields. Threescore men were digging
Down its dark sides for four-and-twenty hours,
Yet in one little week 'twas fill'd to the brim.
This is a sorry pit, and would not hold
Above five hundred full grown corpses. Zounds!
'Tis throwing money away to buy a look
At such a miserable hole as this.

1st Man. I say stand back—what obstinate fool is this
All muffled up to the eyes, with his slouch'd hat
Drawn o'er his face—still pressing to the brink,
As he would have the whole pit to himself
And not allow a peep to one beside.

2d Man. Disturb him not—perhaps he is some wretch
Madden'd by the Plague, and blindly coming here
To bury himself alive, as many do.
Let him leap down, when once he feels the softness
Of the cold bodies yielding under him
He will be right fain, if the steep walls allow,
To crawl back to his life and misery.

3d Man. Let's see thy face. Perhaps thou art afraid
Lest the night air may spoil its delicate beauty.

[*He lifts up the man's hat.*]

Stranger. O scoff not—scoff not at a wretch like me.
My friends! I am no subject for your mirth.

Scene IV.   THE CITY OF THE PLAGUE.

My wife—my father and four little children
Will soon within the dead-cart be brought here,
And I must see them buried spite of laughter,
In spite of laughter, agony, or death.
—Laugh on—laugh on—for all the world is nought
But emptiness and mockery. I myself
Will join your laughter—now I fear it not.
For mirth and misery are but different names
For one delusion.—O that hideous grave
Hath sent its earthy coldness through my being,
And I feel blended with the damp black mould.

    [*He rushes away to a distance, and flings himself*
        down on a tombstone.]

  3*d Man.* Did'st see his face? it was a dreadful sight.
Such face I once remember to have seen
Of a chain'd madman howling in his cell,
Suddenly lifted from the stony floor
It seem'd all eyes—one gleaming of despair.

  1*st Man.* What signifies a living maniac's face?
Have we not often seen th' unsheeted dead
Rear'd up like troops in line against the walls?
To us at distance seemingly alive,
All standing with blotch'd faces, and red eyes
Unclos'd, as in some agonizing dream!

  2*d Man.* Just round the corner of that street—even
    now
I stumbled on such hideous company.
The lamps burn'd dimly, and the tall church-tower

Rose up between me and the moon. I saw
A glimmering whiteness all along the walls
Of several silent houses—up I went—
And right before me stood the ghastly dead
For whose grim faces no kind hand had done
The last sad office. Oh! 'twas terrible!
To recognise in those convulsed features
Friends at whose fire-side I had often sat!
And as I hurried off in shivering fear
Methought I heard a deep and dismal groan
From that long line of mortal visages
Shudder through the deep'ning darkness of the street.

2d Man. Hark—hark!

3d Man. What hideous tolling shakes the city!

1st Man. Methinks the still air, like a sudden wave,
Heaves onward at each slow swing of that bell.
From what tower comes the sound?

2d Man. St Mary Overie's.
I know the toll! a thousand dreams of death
Come with that voice. It fills the den of night
With mortal fear, rendering the silent heavens
The dim abode of unimagined horrors.
List! every heart is beating audibly!

1st Man. Who tolls the bell at the dead hour of night?

2d Man. Perhaps no human hand.

1st Man. 'Tis said one midnight
The sexton heard a tolling from that tower,
And entering on a sudden silently

He saw a being wrapt up in a shroud
Pulling the rope with black and bony hands,
And singing all the while a hideous tune
That breath'd not of this world. It turn'd about,
And one glance of its wild and fiery eye
Crazed the poor wretch's brain.

    2d Man.   **Have mercy—Jesu!**
Dost thou believe in ghosts?

    1st Man.   That midnight bell
Startleth methinks the silent world of spirits.
Who could deny, with that unearthly sound
Tolling through his brain, that something in the grave
Exists more horrible than worms and darkness!
It may be that wild dreams inhabit there,
And disembodied thoughts! Despair—remorse—
And with his stifled shrieks—Insanity!
Half-conscious all the while that the curse of God
Must be eternal, struck into the grave.

    3d Man. That is my creed. Sometimes their chains
        are loosen'd:
How else account for all the sighing sounds
That oft at breathless midnight pass us by,
Wailing with more than mortal agonies.
Strange faces often have been seen at night,
Of persons long entomb'd; and once a phantom
Walk'd to the church-yard with a funeral,
Sobbing and weeping like the Christian crowd,

When as the coffin sank, it disappear'd,
And nought but dry bones lay upon the dust.
 2d Man. What rumbling sound is that?
 3d Man.   The dead-cart comes!
'Tis heavily laden, for it moves but slowly.
It still is in the street—yet o'er the pavement
It sounds as dully as o'er trodden turf.
I have driven a hearse with one dead body in it,
And once by midnight o'er a dreary moor
With no one near me but that sheeted corpse
Till my back felt like ice. But this dead-cart!
See yonder where its lamps, like two great eyes,
Are moving towards us. It comes silently,
For now its wheels are on the church-yard turf.
 [*All make way for it as it approaches the pit.*]
 1st Man. The ghastly idiot-negro, charioteer!
See how he brandishes around his head
A whip that in the yellow lamp-light burns
Like a fiery serpent. How the idiot laughs!
And brightens up his sable countenance,
With his white teeth that stretch from ear to ear.
Thank God he is no Christian—only a negro.
 [*The cart is emptied into the pit.*]
 Stranger. (*leaping in*) Bury me—bury me.
 1st Man.   Let him have his will.
I would not venture down into that pit
To help him out for all that he is worth,
However rich he be.

Scene IV. THE CITY OF THE PLAGUE.

 2d Man.   Yet 'tis a pity
That his watch, and chains, and seals, (they seem'd of
   gold,)
Should thus be lost. I'll leap down instantly
And bring them up, if I'm allow'd to keep them.
   [*The negro when about to drive away the cart de-
    scends, and brings him up with a little dead
    child in his arms.*]
 Stranger. I knew my infant by her shining hair!
Shining at the bottom of the dismal pit
Even like a star in heaven. I hear her breathing!
—Feel, feel this kiss—for I have rescued thee
From being buried alive. My Emmeline,
Open thy blue eyes on thy father's soul.
There's earth upon her face—Oh! wet damp earth
On the warm rosy cheeks of innocence.
Now 'tis kiss'd off for ever. Why not speak?
I will carry thee home unto thy mother's bosom.
There wilt thou speak—wilt laugh and nestle there.
She thought thee dead—but thou art quite alive,
Or rising from the dead—for dead thou art not,
And must not be. Home! home! my Emmeline!
Thy mother waits our coming—home! home! home!
   [*He rushes away with the dead infant in his arms.*]
 1st Man. Well, let him go.—Ha! thanks to the kind
   moon
Coming out so brightly from her tabernacle!
There is a perfect prospect of the pit

Down to the very bottom. Now again
'Tis dark as pitch. Hear! hear the crumbling earth,
How sullenly it sounds when it has reached
The ground-rock! 'Tis indeed a fearful depth!
   [*A small procession enters the church-yard—Voices
   heard singing a dirge for the dead.*]

REVELATIONS, ch. xiv. verse 13.

I heard a voice from heaven
   Say, " Blessed is the doom
" Of them whose trust is in the Lord,
   " When sinking to the tomb!"

The holy spirit spake—
   And I his words repeat—
" Blessed are they"—for after toil
   To mortals rest is sweet.

[*The procession advances*—WILMOT, PRIEST, *&c.
bearing* FRANKFORT's *dead body.*]

Wil. There rest awhile upon this stone, dear corpse.
I with my own hands now will dig thy grave.
Oh! when that grave is filled—what solitude
All earth will seem to me!

Voice from the Crowd.   List to the Priest!

Priest. We all are sinful—and thy soul partook
In the frailties of our fall'n humanity.
Therefore I pray forgiveness to thy sins
From God and Christ. But this I dare to say,
In the dread calm of this wide burial-ground,

That, far as man's heart can be known to man,
A braver, gentler, purer, loftier spirit
Ne'er walk'd this world of trial.—O dear youth!
Sweet boy! beloved from thine infancy!
Methinks I see thee on thy mother's knee
Conning thy evening prayer. Art thou the same,
That, with thy bright hair thus dishevelled,
Liest on a tombstone, dead and coffinless,
About to sink for ever from our eyes!
—One little month—and all thy earthly part
Moulder'd away to nothing—darkly mixed
With a great city-churchyard's dismal mould!
Where sleep in undistinguishable dust,
Young, old, good, wicked, beauteous and deformed,
Trodden under feet by ev'ry worthless thing
Human and brute! in dumb oblivion
Laugh'd over daily by the passing crowd,
Fresh shoals of wretches toiling for this world.
—Wilmot! 'tis hard to lay into the grave
A countenance so benign! a form that walk'd
But yesterday so stately o'er the earth!

Wil. Long as he lay upon his bed, he seem'd
Only a beauteous being stretch'd in sleep
And I could look on him. But lying there,
Shroudless and coffinless beside his grave!····
——Is it religious, Father! thus to weep
O'er a dead body! sure his soul in heaven
Must smile, (how well I know his tender smile)

To see his friends in senseless misery
Thus clinging to the dust.

   Priest.   His soul in heaven
Looks down with love on such a friend as thou!
Here take a blessing with these wither'd hands
Laid on thy honour'd head. Thou wert a friend
In the calm weather of prosperity,—
And then the beauty of friendship shew'd in thee,
Like a glad bark that by her consort's side
Moved through the music of the element,
A sunny cloud of sail. That consort sank—
And now that lonely bark throughout the gloom,
Labours with shatter'd masts, and sore-rent sails,
Not without glory—though she could not save!
Forgive such image—but I see before me
A living sailor and his best dead friend,
And my soul dreams of the sea.

   Wil.   Oh! who comes here!
[*Enter* MAGDALENE *distractedly, followed by* ISABEL *and the* CHILD.]

   Magd. I heard a voice ring through my dreaming ear,
" Haste Magdalene! to the church-yard—they are burying
" Thine own beloved Frankfort!" Tell me where
Your cruel hands have laid my mariner?
He shall not lie in the cold grave to-night
All by himself—Lo! I his bride am here,

And I will kiss his lips, even if the worm
Should be my rival.   I will rest my head
Upon his breast than icy tombstone colder !
Aye ! the grave shall be my happy nuptial bed
Curtain'd with black walls of the dripping clay.
Where is he ? wretches ! have ye buried him ?

 Isabel. Oh ! must I tell thee—Magdalene ! to look round,
That thou mayest see thy Frankfort lying dead !
Behold thy sailor !

   [*Magdalene flings herself down on the body.*]

 Magd.   Art thou still on earth !
O cold, cold kisses ! pale and breathless lips !
Are those sweet eyes indeed for ever clos'd !
—See ! see ! the garb in which he sail'd the deep !
—Thy voyaging all is o'er—thy harbour here !
Anchor'd thou art in everlasting rest,
While over thee the billows of this world
Are with unheeded fury raving on.

 Isabel. Hast thou one word for Isabel ?

 Magd.   My sister !
My love for thee was perfect—Wilmot ! Wilmot !
What art thou doing with that savage spade ?
Ha ! digging Frankfort's grave !—They shall not bury thee !
A thing so beautiful must not be buried ....

     [*She faints upon the body.*]

Wilmot to the Priest. I leave the dying Lady to your
    care.
My soul is strong in agony of love
And unexampled sorrow—and since I
Did undertake to dig my brother's grave,
I will go on with it, until I reach
His mother's coffin!

Voice from the Crowd. God will be his help.
That one small grave—that one dead mariner—
That dying Lady—and those wond'rous friends
So calm, so lofty, yet compassionate—
Do strike a deeper awe into our souls,
A deeper human grief than yon wide pit
With its unnumber'd corpses.

Another Voice. Woe and death
Have made that Angel bright their prey at last!
But yesterday I saw her heavenly face
Becalm a shrieking room with one sweet smile!
For her, old age will tear his hoary locks,
And childhood murmur forth her holy name
Weeping in sorrowful dreams!

Another Voice. Her soft hand clos'd
My children's eyes,—and when she turn'd to go,
The beauty of her weeping countenance
So sank into my heart, that I beheld
The little corpses with a kind of joy,
Assured by that compassionate Angel's smile
That they had gone to heaven.

Magd. (recovering from her swoon.) 'Tis cold ! cold !
cold !
Colder than any living thing can bear !
—Have I been visiting my parents' grave,
And fainted on a tombstone ? Who lies here ?
—Frankfort what ails thee ?

Isabel. Magdalene ! Magdalene !

Magd. Art thou the shadow of a blessed friend
Still living on the earth ?

Isabel. These tombstones tell ·····
And all these pale and mortal visages·····

Magd. Is there a funeral ?

Wilmot. Once I had a brother,
But we have come to lay him in his grave !

Magd. No more ! no more !

Priest. The darkness leaves her
brain !

Magd. All pain, all sorrow, and all earthly fear,
Have left me now, and ye behold me lying
In a deep joy beyond all happiness !
This corpse is beautiful, but 'tis only dust,
And with this last embrace it is forgotten,
And no more is among my dying thoughts.

Priest. How her face kindles with the parting soul !

Magd. O gracious God ! how sweet ! how most de-
lightful
To fade away into eternity
With a clear soul !—So have I seen the shore—

The soft green shore of my own native lake
'Mid sunshine blended with the sleeping waters,
In unobserved union fair and still!
O blessed lake!····think of me Isabel
When thou art walking with that happy child
Through its birch woods, or by yon whispering pines—
Farewell!····that image····Isabel! farewell!

Wil. So clear a voice can ne'er be that of death!
She is recovering.

Magd.   Isabel! look there!
Are those my Parents smiling at my side!
Fold your wings over me—gone—gone to heaven
Are the bright Seraphs!—Christ receive my soul!

                                    [*She dies.*]

Priest. An Angel's pen must write thy epitaph.

Wil. Awful seems human nature in the tears
That old age weeps.

Priest.   Forgive such tears!—So young,
So beautiful amid the opening world,
Who would not weep for them!

Isabel.   The world will weep,
All the wide world will weep!—I have been sitting
On a high cloud above this woeful city,
With a bright angel at my side. She falls
Down from that sunny region, and my soul
Is wandering now in helpless solitude
Through miseries once seen far below my feet!

Priest. Oh! hers will be a memorable name,

Famous in this city—over all the isle
Devoutly breathed in hymns,—and oft invoked
In lofty songs and odes to charity,—
Sacred to childhood in its weeping dreams,
By love—and sorrow—and pity saved for ever
From dark oblivion, like the holy name
Of tutelary Saint.

Isabel. (with energy.) Aye! it will live
Among her native mountains—to all hearts
Familiar music—and the holy house
Where she was born will oft be visited
By mute adorers, and its very dust,
When time hath worn the lowly walls away,
Untrod be held in endless reverence.
Not unforgotten in our shepherds' songs
The maid who far-off perish'd in the Plague!
The glens so well-belov'd will oft repeat
The echo of her name; and all in white
An Angel will be seen to walk the vallies,
Smiling with a face too beauteous to be fear'd
On lonely maiden walking home at night
Across the moonlight hills!

Priest. O faithful Isabel!
Is not this church-yard now a place of peace?

Isabel. Of perfect peace. My spirit looks with eyes
Into the world to come. There Magdalene sits
With them she lov'd on earth.—O mortal body

In faded beauty stretch'd upon the dust,
I love thee still as if thou wert a soul!......
   Priest. Friends let us lift the body.
   Isabel.   In my arms,
Upon my bosom—close unto my heart
Thus do I lift my Magdalene to her grave!
I kiss her brow—her cheeks—her lips—her eye-lids—
Her most delightful hair! I twine my arms
Around her blessed neck—cold cold as ice!
I feel her whole frame in my sorrowful soul.
   Priest. Wilmot! assist our friend......
   Wil. (Starting.)   The sound of waves
Came for one moment o'er my friendless soul.
   Child. O might I go to sleep within the grave
With one so beautiful! No ghost would come
To frighten me on such a breast as this.
The church-yard even at midnight would appear
A place where one might sleep with happy dreams
Where such an angel lay. O might I die
Singing the hymn last night I heard her sing,
And go with her to heaven.
   Isabel.   Heaven bless the child!
Yes! thou art blest in weeping innocence.
   Wil. Here is the prayer-book clasp'd in Magdalene's
      hand,
Let us kneel down while thy blest voice is reading
The funeral-service.

Isabel.   Oh! that fatal day
On which we left our cottage! Magdalene smiled····
Oh! that sweet gleam of sunshine on the lake!····
  Priest. Are we all prepar'd to hear the service read?
  Isabel. All! Come thou sweet child! kneel thou at
        my side!
Hush! sob not—for they now are Spirits in heaven!

END OF THE CITY OF THE PLAGUE.

MISCELLANEOUS POEMS.

THE CHILDREN'S DANCE.

How calm and beautiful the frosty Night
Has stol'n unnotic'd like the hush of sleep
O'er Grassmere-vale! Beneath the mellowing light,
How sinks in softness every rugged steep!
The old Church-tower a solemn watch doth keep,
O'er the sweet Village she adorns so well;
Faintly the freezing stream is heard to weep,
Wild-murmuring far within its icy cell,
And hark! across the Lake, clear chimes the Chapel-
——bell.

Soon will the Moon and all her Stars be here:
A stealing light proclaims her o'er yon hill!
Slowly she raiseth up her radiant sphere,
And stillness, at her smile, becomes more still.
My heart forgets all thoughts of human ill,
And man seems happy as his place of birth:
All things that yield him joy my spirit fill
With kindred joy; and ev'n his humblest mirth
Seems, at this peaceful hour, to beautify the Earth.

THE CHILDREN'S DANCE.

Beyond this vale my fancy may not fly,
Held by its circle in a magic chain;
Of merry-making, and festivity,
Even 'mid this moonlight-scene, shall be my strain.
Nor gracious Nature! when I wake again
A hymn of loftier temper in thy praise,
Wilt thou the Poet's homage-song disdain,—
For Thou hast never listened to his lays,
Who lov'd not lowly life and all its simple ways.

Through many a vale how rang each snow-roof'd cot,
This livelong day with rapture blithe and wild!
All thoughts but of the lingering eve forgot,
Both by grave Parent, and light-hearted Child.
Hail to the Night! whose image oft beguiled
Youth's transient sadness with a startling cheer!
The *Ball-night* this by younkers proudly styled!
The joy at distance bright, burns brighter near—
Now smiles the happiest hour of all their happy year!

All day the earthen floors have felt their feet
Twinkling quick measures to the liquid sound
Of their own small-piped voices shrilly sweet,—
As hand in hand they wheel'd their giddy round.
Ne'er fairy-revels on the greensward mound
To dreaming bard a lovelier shew display'd:—
Titania's self did ne'er with lighter bound

Dance o'er the diamonds of the dewy glade,
Than danc'd, at peep of morn, mine own dear moun-
    tain-maid.

Oft in her own small mirror had the gleam,
The soften'd gleam of her rich golden hair,
That o'er her white neck floated in a stream,
Kindled to smiles that Infant's visage fair,
Half-conscious she that beauty glistened there!
Oft had she glanced her restless eyes aside
On silken sash so bright and debonnair,
Then to her mother flown with leaf-like glide,
Who kiss'd her cherub-head with tears of silent pride.

But all these glad rehearsals now are o'er,
And young and old in many a glittering throng,
By tinkling copse-wood, and hill-pathway pour,
Cheering the air with laughter and with song.
Those first arriv'd think others tarrying long,
And chide them smiling with a friendly jeer,
" To let the music waste itself was wrong,
" So stirringly it strikes upon the ear,
" The lame might dance," they cry, " the aged-deaf
    might hear."

And lo! the crowded ball-room is alive
With restless motion, and a humming noise,
Like on a warm spring-morn a sunny hive,
When round their Queen the waking bees rejoice

THE CHILDREN'S DANCE.

Sweet blends with graver tones the silvery voice
Of children rushing eager to their seats;
The Master proud of his fair flock employs
His guiding beck that due attention meets,—
List! through the silent room each anxious bosom beats!

Most beautiful and touching is the scene!
More blissful far to me than Fancy's bower!
Arch'd are the walls with wreaths of holly green,
Whose dark-red berries blush beside the flower
That kindly comes to charm the wintry hour,
The Christmas rose! the glory white as snow!
The dusky roof seems brighten'd by the power
Of bloom and verdure mingling thus below,
Whence many a taper-light sends forth a cheerful glow.

There sit together, tranquilly arrayed,
The Friends and Parents of the infant-band.
A Mother nodding to her timid maid
With cheering smiles—or beckoning with her hand,
A sign of love the child doth understand.
There, deeper thoughts the Father's heart employ:
His features grave with fondness melting-bland,
He asks his silent heart, with gushing joy,
If all the vale can match his own exulting Boy.

See! where in blooming rows the children sit—
All loving partners by the idle floor

As yet divided—save where boy doth flit,
Lightly as small wave running 'long the shore,
To whisper something, haply said before,
Unto the soft cheek of his laughing May!
The whiles the master eyes the opening door—
And, fearing longer than one smile to stay,
Turns on his noiseless heel, and jocund wheels away.

O Band of living Flowers! O taintless wreathe!
By nature nourish'd 'mid her mountain air!
O sweet unfolding buds, that blush and breathe
Of innocence and love! I scarce may dare
To gaze upon you!—What soft gleams of hair!
What peaceful foreheads! and what heavenly eyes!
Bosoms so sweet will never harbour care;
Such spiritual breath was never made for sighs!
For you still breathe on Earth the gales of Paradise.

But I will call you by your human name,—
Children of Earth, of Frailty, and Distress!
Alternate objects ye of praise and blame!
The spell is broken—do I love you less?
Ah! no!—a deep'ning, mournful tenderness
Yearns at my heart, e'en now when I behold
What trivial joys the human soul can bless!
I feel a pathos that can ne'er be told
Breath'd from yon *mortal* locks of pure ethereal gold.

THE CHILDREN'S DANCE.

Where now that angel face—that fairy frame—
The joyful beauty of that burnish'd head
That shining forth o'er all—a star-like flame—
Once through this room admiring rapture shed!
Can that fair breast so full of life be dead!
All mute those ruddy lips whose dewy balm
As if through breathing flowers sweet music shed!
Those bounding limbs chain'd now in endless calm—
—For her last Sabbath-day was sung the funeral psalm!

One reverend head I miss amid the throng—
'Tis bowed in sorrow o'er his cottage hearth!
The tread of dancing feet—the voice of song—
The gladsome viol—and the laugh of mirth
To him seem mockery on this lonesome earth.
Rich in one child—he felt as if his store
Of bliss might never yield to mortal dearth—
But dry the cup of joy that once ran o'er!
—Now that grey-headed man is poorest of the poor.

That was a stirring sound—my heart feels light
Once more, and happy as a lamb at play.
At music such as this—pale thought takes flight—
It speaks of Scotland too—a dear strathspey!
No vulgar skill the Master doth display—
The living bow leaps dancing o'er the strings—
The wrinkled face of Age is bright as day—

While each glad child in fancied measure springs,
And feels as if through air he skimm'd on flying wings.

A hush of admiration chains the breath,
And calms the laughing features of us all;
The room, erewhile so loud, is still as death—
For lo! the Infant-monarchs of the ball
Rise from their seats, rejoicing at the call,
And move soft-gliding to their proper place!
He in his triumph rising straight and tall;
She light of air, and delicate of face,
More bright through fear's faint shade her wild uncon-
    scious grace.

Towards each other their delighted eyes
They smiling turn, and all, at once, may tell
From their subdued and sinless ecstasies
That these fair children love each other well.
They sport and play in the same native dell,
There, each lives happy in a shelter'd nest;
And though the children of our vales excel
In touching beauty—far above the rest
Shine forth this starlike pair—the loveliest and the best.

Like a faint shadow falls the pride of youth
O'er faces sparkling yet with childhood's light—
Joy, friendship, fondness, innocence and truth,
That blushing maiden to her Boy unite

THE CHILDREN'S DANCE.

More than a brother dear! Aye—this glad night
Across their quiet souls will often move,
A spot of vernal sunshine ever bright!
When through youth's fairy-land no more they rove,
And feel that Grief oft sits beside her sister Love.—

But lo! their graceful salutations lend
A mutual boldness to each beating heart;
Up strikes the tune—suspense is at an end—
Like fearless forest-fawns away they start!
How wildly nature now combines with art!
The motions of the infant mountaineer,
Wont o'er the streams and up the hills to dart
Subdued by precept and by music here,
Enthral the admiring soul at once through eye and ear!

Like sunbeams glancing o'er a meadow-field,
From side to side the airy spirits swim.
What keen and kindling rapture shines reveal'd
Around their eyes, and moves in every limb!
See! how they twine their flexile arms so slim,
In graceful arches o'er their hanging hair,
Whose ringlets for a while their eyes bedim.
The music stops—they stand like statues there—
Then parting glide away on noiseless steps of air.

And now a ready hand hath round them thrown
A flowing garland, for their beauteous Queen

THE CHILDREN'S DANCE.

Wreath'd by her playmates—roses newly blown
White-clustering 'mid the ivy's vivid green.
Enfolded thus in innocence, they lean
Their silky heads in inclination dear,
Their blent locks fluttering through the space between,—
And do they not, advancing thus, appear
Like Angels sent by Spring to usher in the year?

Their movements every instant lighter grow.
Motion to them more easy seems than rest:
Their cheeks are tinged with a diviner glow—
Their gleaming locks a perfect bliss attest.
Now is the triumph of their art confest
By rising murmurs, and soft-rustling feet,
All round th' admiring room—they cease—opprest
With a pride-mingled shame—and to their seat
Fly off, 'mid thundering praise, with bosoms fluttering
 sweet.

Around their Queen her loving playmates press,
Proud of her dancing, as it were their own;
With voices trembling through their tenderness,
Like to the flute's low tones when sweetly blown!
Envy to their pure breasts is yet unknown;
Too young and happy for a moment's guile!
There Innocence still sacred keeps her throne,
Well-pleas'd, in that calm hold, to see the while
Lingering on human lips an unpolluted smile.

THE CHILDREN'S DANCE.

Ah me! that Bards in many a lovely lay,
Forgetting all their own delightful years,
Should sing that life is but one little day,
And this most blessed world the vale of tears!
Even in such songs mysterious truth appears:
We weep—forget—or muse resign'd on death—
But oh! that those inevitable years
The soul should sully with bedimming breath,
And prove how vain a dream is all our childhood's faith!

Go to thy mother's arms thou blessed thing!
And in her yearning bosom hide thy head:
Behold! how bliss resembleth sorrowing!
When smiles are glistening—why should tears be shed!
Nor, grey-hair'd man! art thou dishonoured
By those big drops that force at last their way
Down thy grave wrinkled face—when thou art dead,
That child thou knowest will weep upon thy clay—
Thus fathers oft are sad when those they love are gay.

But why should merriment thus feel alloy,
Sanction'd by Nature though such sadness be?
—Look on yon Figure! how he swells with joy!
With head-erecting pride and formal glee!
And may a Poet dare to picture thee,
As stiff thou walk'st thy pupils sly among;
While roguish elf doth ape thy pedantry?
Loudly, I trow, would bark the critic throng,
If vulgar name like thine should slip into my song.

THE CHILDREN'S DANCE.

And yet thou shalt not go without the meed
Of well-earn'd praise—one tributary line:
And haply as I tune my simple reed,
Such theme the pastoral muse may not decline.
Nor vain nor useless is a task like thine—
That, ere the gleams of life's glad morning fly,
Bids native grace with fresh attractions shine,
Taming the wild—emboldening the shy—
And still its end the same—the bliss of infancy!

Nor think the coldest spirit could withstand
The genial influence breath'd, like balm from heaven,
From rosy childhood, in a vernal band
Dancing before him every happy Even.
When through the gloom their gliding forms are driven,
Like soft stars hurrying through the airy mist,
Unto his heart paternal dreams are given,
And in the bliss of innocent beauty blest,
Oft hath that simple man their burnish'd ringlets kist.

No idle, worthless, wandering man is he,
But in this vale of honest parents bred:
Train'd to a life of patient industry,
He with the lark in summer leaves his bed,
Through the sweet calm by morning twilight shed,
Walking to labour by that cheerful song.
And, making now pure pleasure of a trade,

THE CHILDREN'S DANCE.

When Winter comes, with nights so dark and long,
'Tis his to train to grace the smiling infant throng.

And he, I ween, is aye a welcome guest
In every cottage-home on hill and vale;
And oft by matron grave is warmly prest
To honour with his praise her home-brew'd ale.
Smiles the grown maid her master to regale,
Mindful of all his kindness when a child,
Invited thus, the master may not fail
To laud with fitting phrase the liquor mild,
And prays that heaven may bless the cottage on the
    wild.

O fair the mazy dance that breaks my dream!
Heaven dawns upon me as I starting wake!
A flight of fancy this—a frolic whim—
A mirthful tumult in which all partake.
So dance the sunny atoms o'er a lake;
So small clouds blend together in the sky;
So when the evening gales the grove forsake,
The radiant lime-leaves twinkle yet on high,
So flutter new-fledg'd birds to their own melody.

Through bright confusion order holds her reign,
And not one infant there but well doth know
By cunning rules her station to regain,

And fearless of mistakes to come and go.
Yet did the master no deep pains bestow
On these small Elves so docile, and so true
To tune and figure. Nature will'd it so,
Who fram'd to grace their stature as it grew,
And train'd their fairy feet among the morning dew.

True that, in polish'd life, refinement sheds
A fragile elegance o'er childhood's frame,—
And in a trembling lustre steeps their heads,
A finer charm, a grace without a name.
There, culture kindly breathes on nature's flame;
And angel beauty owns her genial sway.
But oh! too oft doth dove-eyed Pity claim
The unconscious victims dancing light and gay,
For sickness lends that bloom, the symbol of decay.

Here Health, descending from her mountain-throne,
Surveys with rapture yon delighted train
Of rosy Sprites, by day and night her own,
Though mortal creatures, strangers yet to pain!
For she hath taught them up the hills to strain,
Following her foot-prints o'er the dewy flowers,
Light as the shadows flitting o'er the plain,
Soon as the earth salutes the dawning hours
With song and fragrance pour'd from all her glitt'ring
    bowers.

THE CHILDREN'S DANCE.

Nor deem to gilded roofs alone confin'd
The magic charm of manners mild and free;
Attendant mostly they on peace of mind,
Best cherish'd by the breath of purity.
Yea! oft in scenes like this of rustic glee,
Where youth, and joy, and innocence resort,
The *Manners* gladly rule the revelry,
Unseen, they mingle in the quickening sport,
Well pleased 'mid village-hinds to hold their homely
    court.

See! with what tenderness of mien, voice, eye,
Yon little stripling, scarce twelve summers old,
Detains his favourite partner gliding by,
Becoming, as she smiles, more gaily bold!
'Tis thus the pleasures of our youth unfold
The fairest feelings of the human heart;
Nor, o'er our heads when silvering years are rolled,
Will the fond image from our fancy part,
But clings tenacious there 'mid passion, pride, and art.

Aye! nights like this are felt o'er many a vale!
Their sweet remembrance mocks the drifted snow
That chokes the cottage up,—it bids the hail
With cheerful pattering 'gainst the panes to blow.
Hence, if the town-bred traveller chance to go
Into the mountain-dwellings of our poor,
The peasants greet with unembarrass'd brow

The splendid stranger honouring thus their door,
And lead his steps with grace along the rushy floor.

But now the lights are waxing dim and pale,
And shed a fitful gleaming o'er the room ;
'Mid the dim hollies one by one they fail,
Another hour, and all is wrapt in gloom.
And lo! without, the cold, bright stars illume
The cloudless air, so beautiful and still,
While proudly placed in her meridian dome
Night's peerless Queen the realms of heaven doth fill
With peace and joy, and smiles on each vast slumbering
　　　hill.

The dance and music cease their blended glee,
And many a wearied infant hangs her head,
Dropping asleep upon her mother's knee,
Worn out with joy, and longing for her bed.
Yet some lament the bliss too quickly fled,
And fain the dying revels would prolong—
Loth that the parting " Farewell," should be said,
They round the Master in a circle throng,—
Unmoved, alas! he stands their useless prayers among.

And now an old man asks him, ere they go,
If willing he a parting tune to play—
One of those Scottish tunes so sweet and slow !
And proud is he such wishes to obey.

Then " Auld lang syne" the wild and mournful lay
Ne'er breathed through human hearts unmoved by
    tears,
Wails o'er the strings, and wailing dies away !
While tremblingly his mellow voice he rears,
Ah me ! the aged weep to think of former years !

Now rising to depart, each Parent pays
Some compliment well-suited to his ear—
Couch'd, through their warmth of heart, in florid phrase,
Yet, by a parent's honest hopes, sincere !
They trust to meet him all another year,
If gracious heaven to them preserve the boon
Of life and health—and now with tranquil cheer,
Their hearts still touched with that delightful tune,
Homeward they wend along beneath the silent moon.

O'er Loughrig-cliffs I see one party climb,
Whose empty dwellings through the hush'd midnight
Sleep in the shade of Langdale-pikes sublime—
Up Dummail-Raise, unmindful of the height,
His daughter in his arms, with footsteps light
The father walks, afraid lest she should wake !
Through lonely Easdale past yon cots so white
On Helm-crag side, their journey others take ;
And some to those sweet homes that smile by Rydal
    lake.

He too, the Poet of this humble show,
Silent walks homeward through the hour of rest—
While quiet as the depth of spotless snow,
A pensive calm contentment fills his breast!
O wayward man! were he not truly blest!
That Lake so still below—that Sky above!
Unto his heart a sinless Infant prest,
Whose ringlets like the glittering dew-wire move,
Floating and sinking soft amid the breath of love!

ADDRESS
TO A
WILD DEER
IN THE FOREST OF DALNESS, GLEN-ETIVE, AR-
GYLLSHIRE.

Magnificent Creature! so stately and bright!
In the pride of thy spirit pursuing thy flight;
For what hath the child of the desert to dread,
Wafting up his own mountains that far-beaming head;
Or borne like a whirlwind down on the vale?—
—Hail! King of the wild and the beautiful!—hail!
Hail! Idol divine!—whom Nature hath borne
O'er a hundred hill-tops since the mists of the morn,
Whom the pilgrim lone wandering on mountain and
    moor,
As the vision glides by him, may blameless adore;
For the joy of the happy, the strength of the free
Are spread in a garment of glory o'er thee.

Up! up to yon cliff! like a King to his throne!
O'er the black silent forest pil'd lofty and lone—

A throne which the eagle is glad to resign
Unto footsteps so fleet and so fearless as thine.
There the bright heather springs up in love of thy
     breast—
Lo! the clouds in the depth of the sky are at rest,
And the race of the wild winds is o'er on the hill!
In the hush of the mountains, ye antlers lie still—
Though your branches now toss in the storm of delight,
Like the arms of the pine on yon shelterless height.
One moment—thou bright Apparition!—delay!
Then melt o'er the crags, like the sun from the day.

Aloft on the weather-gleam, scorning the earth,
The wild spirit hung in majestical mirth:
In dalliance with danger, he bounded in bliss,
O'er the fathomless gloom of each moaning abyss;
O'er the grim rocks careering with prosperous motion,
Like a ship by herself in full sail o'er the ocean!
Then proudly he turn'd ere he sank to the dell,
And shook from his forehead a haughty farewell,
While his horns in a crescent of radiance shone,
Like a flag burning bright when the vessel is gone.

The ship of the desert hath pass'd on the wind,
And left the dark ocean of mountains behind!
But my spirit will travel wherever she flee,
And behold her in pomp o'er the rim of the sea—

Her voyage pursue—till her anchor be cast
In some cliff-girdled haven of beauty at last.

What lonely magnificence stretches around!
Each sight how sublime! and how awful each sound!
All hush'd and serene, as a region of dreams,
The mountains repose 'mid the roar of the streams,—
Their glens of black umbrage by cataracts riven,
But calm their blue tops in the beauty of Heaven.
Here the glory of nature hath nothing to fear—
—Aye! Time the destroyer in power hath been here;
And the forest that hung on yon mountain so high,
Like a black thunder cloud on the arch of the sky,
Hath gone, like that cloud, when the tempest came by.
Deep sunk in the black moor, all worn and decay'd,
Where the floods have been raging, the limbs are dis-
  play'd
Of the Pine-tree and Oak sleeping vast in the gloom,—
The kings of the forest disturb'd in their tomb.

E'en now, in the pomp of their prime, I behold
O'erhanging the desart the forests of old!
So gorgeous their verdure, so solemn their shade,
Like the heavens above them, they never may fade.
The sunlight is on them—in silence they sleep—
A glimmering glow, like the breast of the deep,
When the billows scarce heave in the calmness of morn.
—Down the pass of Glen-Etive the tempest is borne,—

ADDRESS TO A WILD DEER.

And the hill side is swinging, and roars with a sound
In the heart of the forest embosom'd profound.
Till all in a moment the tumult is o'er,
And the mountain of thunder is still as the shore
When the sea is at ebb; not a leaf nor a breath
To disturb the wild solitude, steadfast as death.

From his eyrie the eagle hath soar'd with a scream,
And I wake on the edge of the cliff from my dream;
—Where now is the light of thy far-beaming brow?
Fleet son of the wilderness! where art thou now?
—Again o'er yon crag thou return'st to my sight,
Like the horns of the moon from a cloud of the night!
Serene on thy travel—as soul in a dream—
Thou needest no bridge o'er the rush of the stream.
With thy presence the pine-grove is fill'd, as with light,
And the caves, as thou passest, one moment are bright.
Through the arch of the rainbow that lies on the rock
'Mid the mist stealing up from the cataract's shock,
Thou fling'st thy bold beauty, exulting and free,
O'er a pit of grim blackness, that roars like the sea.

—His voyage is o'er!—As if struck by a spell
He motionless stands in the hush of the dell,
There softly and slowly sinks down on his breast,
In the midst of his pastime enamour'd of rest.
A stream in a clear pool that endeth its race—
A dancing ray chain'd to one sunshiny place—

A cloud by the winds to calm solitude driven—
A hurricane dead in the silence of heaven!

Fit couch of repose for a pilgrim like thee!
Magnificent prison enclosing the free!
With rock-wall encircled—with precipice crown'd—
Which, awoke by the sun, thou can'st clear at a bound.
'Mid the fern and the heather kind Nature doth keep
One bright spot of green for her favourite's sleep;
And close to that covert, as clear as the skies
When their blue depths are cloudless, a little lake lies,
Where the creature at rest can his image behold
Looking up through the radiance, as bright and as bold!
How lonesome! how wild! yet the wildness is rife
With the stir of enjoyment—the spirit of life.
The glad fish leaps up in the heart of the lake,
Whose depths, at the sullen plunge, sullenly quake!
Elate on the fern-branch the grasshopper sings,
And away in the midst of his roundelay springs;
'Mid the flowers of the heath, not more bright than
    himself,
The wild-bee is busy, a musical elf—
Then starts from his labour, unwearied and gay,
And, circling the antlers, booms far far away.
While high up the mountains, in silence remote,
The cuckoo unseen is repeating his note,
And mellowing echo, on watch in the skies,
Like a voice from some loftier climate replies.

ADDRESS TO A WILD DEER.

With wide-branching antlers a guard to his breast,
There lies the wild Creature, even stately in rest!
'Mid the grandeur of nature, compos'd and serene,
And proud in his heart of the mountainous scene,
He lifts his calm eye to the eagle and raven,
At noon sinking down on smooth wings to their haven,
As if in his soul the bold Animal smil'd
To his friends of the sky, the joint-heirs of the wild.

Yes! fierce looks thy nature, ev'n hush'd in repose—
In the depth of thy desert regardless of foes.
Thy bold antlers call on the hunter afar
With a haughty defiance to come to the war!
No outrage is war to a creature like thee!
The bugle-horn fills thy wild spirit with glee,
As thou bearest thy neck on the wings of the wind,
And the laggardly gaze-hound is toiling behind.
In the beams of thy forehead that glitter with death,
In feet that draw power from the touch of the heath,—
In the wide-raging torrent that lends thee its roar,—
In the cliff that once trod must be trodden no more,—
Thy trust—'mid the dangers that threaten thy reign!
—But what if the stag on the mountain be slain?
On the brink of the rock—lo! he standeth at bay
Like a victor that falls at the close of the day—
While hunter and hound in their terror retreat
From the death that is spurn'd from his furious feet:

And his last cry of anger comes back from the skies,
As nature's fierce son in the wilderness dies.

High life of a hunter! he meets on the hill
The new waken'd daylight, so bright and so still;
And feels, as the clouds of the morning unroll,
The silence, the splendour, ennoble his soul.
'Tis his o'er the mountains to stalk like a ghost,
Enshrouded with mist, in which nature is lost,
Till he lifts up his eyes, and flood, valley, and height,
In one moment all swim in an ocean of light;
While the sun, like a glorious banner unfurl'd,
Seems to wave o'er a new, more magnificent world.
'Tis his—by the mouth of some cavern his seat—
The lightning of heaven to hold at his feet,
While the thunder below him, that growls from the cloud,
To him comes on echo more awfully loud.
When the clear depth of noon-tide, with glittering motion,
O'erflows the lone glens—an aërial ocean—
When the earth and the heavens, in union profound,
Lie blended in beauty that knows not a sound—
As his eyes in the sunshiny solitude close
'Neath a rock of the desert in dreaming repose,
He sees, in his slumbers, such visions of old
As his wild Gaelic songs to his infancy told;

O'er the mountains a thousand plum'd hunters are borne,
And he starts from his dream at the blast of the horn.

Yes! child of the desert! fit quarry were thou
For the hunter that came with a crown on his brow,—
By princes attended with arrow and spear,
In their white-tented camp, for the warfare of deer.
In splendour the tents on the green summit stood,
And brightly they shone from the glade in the wood,
And, silently built by a magical spell,
The pyramid rose in the depth of the dell.
All mute was the palace of Lochy that day,
When the king and his nobles—a gallant array—
To Gleno or Glen-Etive came forth in their pride,
And a hundred fierce stags in their solitude died.
Not lonely and single they pass'd o'er the height—
But thousands swept by in their hurricane-flight;
And bow'd to the dust in their trampling tread
Was the plumage on many a warrior's head.
—" Fall down on your faces!—the herd is at hand!"
—And onwards they came like the sea o'er the sand;
Like the snow from the mountain when loosen'd by
    rain,
And rolling along with a crash to the plain;
Like a thunder-split oak-tree, that falls in one shock
With his hundred wide arms from the top of the rock,
Like the voice of the sky, when the black cloud is near,
So sudden, so loud, came the tempest of Deer.

ADDRESS TO A WILD DEER.

Wild mirth of the desert! fit pastime for kings!
Which still the rude Bard in his solitude sings.
Oh reign of magnificence! vanish'd for ever!
Like music dried up in the bed of a river,
Whose course hath been chang'd! yet my soul can sur-
    vey
The clear cloudless morn of that glorious day.
Yes! the wide silent forest is loud as of yore,
And the far-ebbed grandeur rolls back to the shore.

I wake from my trance!—lo! the Sun is declining!
And the Black-mount afar in his lustre is shining,
—One soft golden gleam ere the twilight prevail!
Then down let me sink to the cot in the dale,
Where sings the fair maid to the viol so sweet,
Or the floor is alive with her white twinkling feet.
Down, down like a bird to the depth of the dell!
—Vanish'd Creature! I bid thy far image farewell!

THE

VOICE OF DEPARTED FRIENDSHIP.

I HAD a Friend who died in early youth !
—And often in those melancholy dreams,
When my soul travels through the umbrage deep
That shades the silent world of memory,
Methinks I hear his voice ! Sweet as the breath
Of balmy ground-flowers stealing from some spot
Of sunshine sacred, in a gloomy wood,
To everlasting spring.
     In the church-yard
Where now he sleeps—the day before he died,
Silent we sat together on a grave ;
Till gently laying his pale hand on mine,
Pale in the moonlight that was coldly sleeping
On heaving sod and marble monument,—
This was the music of his last farewell !
" Weep not my brother ! though thou seest me led
" By short and easy stages, day by day,

" With motion almost imperceptible
" Into the quiet grave.   God's will be done.
" Even when a boy, in doleful solitude
" My soul oft sat within the shadow of death !
" And when I look'd along the laughing earth,
" Up the blue heavens, and through the middle air
" Joyfully ringing with the sky-lark's song,
" I wept ! and thought how sad for one so young
" To bid farewell to so much happiness.
" But Christ hath call'd me from this lower world,
" Delightful though it be—and when I gaze
" On the green earth and all its happy hills,
" 'Tis with such feelings as a man beholds
" A little Farm which he is doom'd to leave
" On an appointed day.   Still more and more
" He loves it as that mournful day draws near,
" But hath prepar'd his heart—and is resign'd."
—Then lifting up his radiant eyes to heaven,
He said with fervent voice—" O what were life
" Even in the warm and summer-light of joy
" Without those hopes, that like refreshing gales
" At evening from the sea, come o'er the soul
" Breath'd from the ocean of eternity.
" —And oh ! without them who could bear the storms
" That fall in roaring blackness o'er the waters
" Of agitated life ! Then hopes arise
" All round our sinking souls, like those fair birds
" O'er whose soft plumes the tempest hath no power,

" Waving their snow-white wings amid the darkness,
" And wiling us with gentle motion, on
" To some calm island! on whose silvery strand
" Dropping at once, they fold their silent pinions,—
" And as we touch the shores of paradise
" In love and beauty walk around our feet!"

LORD RONALD'S CHILD.

Three days ago Lord Ronald's child
Was singing o'er the mountain-wild,
　　Among the sunny showers
That brought the rainbow to her sight,
And bathed her footsteps in the light
　　Of purple heather-flowers.
But chilly came the evening's breath—
The silent dew was cold with death—
　　She reached her home with pain;
And from the bed where now she lies,
With snow-white face and closed eyes,
　　She ne'er must rise again.

Still is she as a frame of stone,
That in its beauty lies alone,
With silence breathing from its face,
For ever in some holy place!
Chapel or aisle! on marble laid—
With pale hands o'er its pale breast spread—

An image humble, meek and low,
Of one forgotten long ago!

Soft feet are winding up the stair—
And lo! a Vision passing fair!
All dress'd in white—a mournful show—
A band of orphan children come,
With footsteps like the falling snow,
To bear to her eternal home
The gracious Lady who look'd down
With smiles on their forlorn estate—
—But Mercy up to heaven is gone,
And left the friendless to their fate.

They pluck the honeysuckle's bloom,
That through the window fills the room
With mournful odours—and the rose
That in its innocent beauty glows,
Leaning its dewy golden head
Towards the pale face of the dead,
Weeping like a thing forsaken
Unto eyes that will not waken.

All bathed in pity's gentle showers
They place these melancholy flowers
Upon the cold white breast!
And there they lie! profoundly calm!
Ere long to fill with fading balm
A place of deeper rest!

By that fair Band the bier is borne
Into the open light of morn,—
And, till the parting dirge be said,
Upon a spot of sunshine laid
Beneath a grove of trees!
Bowed and uncovered every head—
Bright-tressed youth—and hoary age—
—Then suddenly before the dead
Lord Ronald's gather'd vassalage
Fall down upon their knees!

Glen-Etive and its mountains lie
All silent as the depth profound
Of that unclouded sunbright sky—
—Low heard the melancholy sound
Of waters murmuring by.
—Glides softly from the orphan-band
A weeping Child, and takes her stand
Close to the Lady's feet—
Then wildly sings a funeral hymn!
With overflowing eyes and dim
Fix'd on the winding-sheet!—

HYMN.

O beautiful the streams
  That through our vallies run,
Singing and dancing in the gleams
  Of summer's cloudless sun.

LORD RONALD'S CHILD.

The sweetest of them all
   From its fairy banks is gone;
And the music of the waterfall
   Hath left the silent stone!

Up among the mountains
   In soft and mossy cell,
By the silent springs and fountains
   The happy wild-flowers dwell.

The queen-rose of the wilderness
   Hath wither'd in the wind,
And the shepherds see no loveliness
   In the blossoms left behind.

Birds cheer our lonely groves
   With many a beauteous wing—
When happy in their harmless loves
   How tenderly they sing.

O'er all the rest was heard
   One wild and mournful strain,
—But hush'd is the voice of that hymning bird,
   She ne'er must sing again!

Bright through the yew-trees gloom,
   I saw a sleeping dove!
On the silence of her silvery plume,
   The sunlight lay in love.

LORD RONALD'S CHILD.

The grove seem'd all her own
  Round the beauty of that breast—
—But the startled dove afar is flown!
  Forsaken is her nest!

In yonder forest wide
  A flock of wild-deer lies,
Beauty breathes o'er each tender side,
  And shades their peaceful eyes!

The hunter in the night
  Hath singled out the doe,
In whose light the mountain-flock lay bright,
  Whose hue was like the snow!

A thousand stars shine forth,
  With pure and dewy ray—
Till by night the mountains of our north
  Seem gladdening in the day.

O empty all the heaven!
  Though a thousand lights be there—
For clouds o'er the evening-star are driven,
  And shorn her golden hair!

That melancholy music dies—
And all at once the kneeling crowd
Is stirr'd with groans, and sobs, and sighs—

LORD RONALD'S CHILD.

As sudden blasts come rustling loud
Along the silent skies.
—Hush! hush! the dirge doth breathe again!
The youngest of the orphan train
Walks up unto the bier,
With rosy cheeks, and smiling eyes
As heaven's unclouded radiance clear;
And there like Hope to Sorrow's strain
With dewy voice replies.

   —What! though the stream be dead,
     Its banks all still and dry!
   It murmureth now o'er a lovelier bed
     In the air-groves of the sky.

   What! though our prayers from death
     The queen-rose might not save!
   With brighter bloom and balmier breath
     She springeth from the grave.

   What! though our bird of light
     Lie mute with plumage dim!
   In heaven I see her glancing bright—
     I hear her angel hymn.

   What! though the dark tree smile
     No more—with our dove's calm sleep
   She folds her wing on a sunny isle
     In heaven's untroubled deep!

LORD RONALD'S CHILD.

True that our beauteous doe
    Hath left her still retreat—
But purer now in heavenly snow
    She lies at Jesus' feet.

O star! untimely set!
    Why should we weep for thee!
Thy bright and dewy coronet
    Is rising o'er the sea!

THE WIDOW.

The courtly hall is gleaming bright
With fashion's graceful throng—
All hearts are chain'd in still delight,
For like the heaven-born voice of night
Breathes Handel's sacred song.
Nor on my spirit melts in vain
The deep—the wild—the mournful strain
That fills the echoing hall
(Though many a callous soul be there)
With sighs, and sobs, and cherish'd pain—
—While on a face, as Seraph's fair,
Mine eyes in sadness fall.

Not those the tears that smiling flow
As fancied sorrow bleeds,
Like dew upon the rose's glow;
—That Lady 'mid the glitt'ring show
Is cloth'd in widow's weeds.

THE WIDOW.

She sits in reverie profound,
And drinks and lives upon the sound,
As if she ne'er would wake!
Her clos'd eyes cannot hold the tears
That tell what dreams her soul have bound—
In memory they of other years
For a dead husband's sake.

Methinks her inmost soul lies spread
Before my tearful sight—
A garden whose best flowers are dead,
A sky still fair (though darkened)
With hues of lingering light.
I see the varying feelings chase
Each other o'er her pallid face,
From shade to deepest gloom.
She thinks on living objects dear,
And pleasure lends a chearful grace;
But oh! that look so dim and drear,
—Her heart is in the tomb.

Rivalling the tender crescent Moon
The Star of evening shines—
A warm, still, balmy night of June,
Low-murmuring with a fitful tune
From yonder grove of pines.
In the silence of that starry sky,
Exchanging vows of constancy,

THE WIDOW.

Two happy lovers stray.
—To her how sad and strange! to know,
In darkness while the phantoms fade,
That one a widow'd wretch is now,
The other in the clay.

A wilder gleam disturbs her eye.
Oh! hush the deep'ning strain!
And must the youthful Warrior die?
A gorgeous funeral passes by,
The dead-march stuns her brain.
The singing voice she hears no more,
Across his grave the thunders roar!
How weeps yon gallant band
O'er him their valour could not save!
For the bayonet is red with gore,
And he, the beautiful and brave,
Now sleeps in Egypt's sand.

But far away in cloud and mist
The ghastly vision swims.
—Unto that dying cadence list!
She thinks the voices of the blest
Now chaunt their evening hymns.
O for a dove's unwearied wing,
That she might fly where angels sing
Around the judgment-seat;

That Spirit pure to kiss again,
And smile at earthly sorrowing!
Wash'd free from every mortal stain,
At Jesus' blessed feet.

How longs her spirit to recal
That prayer so vain and wild!
For, idly-wandering round the Hall,
Her eyes are startled as they fall
On her own beauteous Child.
Gazing on one so good and fair,
Less mournful breathes that holy air,
And almost melts to mirth:
Pleas'd will she sojourn here a while,
And see, beneath her pious care,
In heaven's most gracious sunshine smile
The sweetest Flower on earth.

The song dies 'mid the silent strings,
And the Hall is now alive
With a thousand gay and fluttering things;
—The noise to her a comfort brings,
Her heart and soul revive.
With solemn pace and loving pride
She walks by her fair daughter's side,
Who views with young delight
The gaudy sparkling revelry,—
Unconscious that from far and wide

THE WIDOW.

On her is turn'd each charmed eye—
—The Beauty of the night!

A Spirit she! and Joy her name!
She walks upon the air;
Grace swims throughout her fragile frame,
And glistens like a lambent flame
Amid her golden hair.
Her eyes are of the heavenly blue,
A cloudless twilight bathed in dew;
The blushes on her cheek,
Like the roses of the vernal year
That lend the virgin snow their hue—
—And oh! what pure delight to hear
The gentle Vision speak!

Yet dearer than that rosy glow
To me yon cheek so wan;
Lovely I thought it long ago,
But lovelier far now blanch'd with woe
Like the breast-down of the swan.
Then worship ye the sweet—the young—
Hang on the witchcraft of her tongue,
Wild-murmuring like the lute.
On thee O Lady! let me gaze,
Thy soul is now a lyre unstrung,
But I hear the voice of other days,
Though these pale lips be mute.

THE WIDOW.

Lovely thou art! yet none may dare
That placid soul to move.
Most beautiful thy braided hair,
But awful holiness breathes there
Unmeet for earthly love.
More touching far than deep distress
Thy smiles of languid happiness,
That like the gleams of Even
O'er thy calm cheek serenely play.
—Thus at the silent hour we bless,
Unmindful of the joyous day,
The still sad face of Heaven.

SOLITUDE.

O VALE of visionary rest !
—Hush'd as the grave it lies
With heaving banks of tenderest green,
Yet brightly, happily serene,
As cloud-vale of the sleepy west
Reposing on the skies.
Its reigning spirit may not vary—
What change can seasons bring
Unto so sweet, so calm a spot,
Where every loud and restless thing
Is like a far-off dream forgot?
Mild, gentle, mournful, solitary,
As if it aye were spring,
And Nature lov'd to witness here
The still joys of the infant year,
'Mid flowers and music wandering glad,
For ever happy, yet for ever sad.

This little world how still and lone
With that horizon of its own !

SOLITUDE.

And, when in silence falls the night,
With its own Moon how purely bright!
No shepherd's Cot is here—no Shealing
Its verdant roof through trees revealing—
No branchy covert like a nest,
Where the weary woodmen rest,
And their jocund carols sing
O'er the fallen Forest-King.
Inviolate by human hand
The fragrant white-stem'd birch-trees stand,
With many a green and sunny glade
'Mid their embowering murmurs made
By gradual soft decay—
Where stealing to that little lawn
From secret haunt and half-afraid,
The Doe, in mute affection gay,
At close of eve leads forth her fawn
Amid the flowers to play.
And in that dell's soft bosom, lo!
Where smileth up a cheerful glow
Of water pure as air,
A Tarn by two small streamlets spread
In beauty o'er its waveless bed,
Reflecting in that heaven so still
The birch-grove mid-way up the hill,
And summits green and bare.

How lone! beneath its veil of dew
That morning's rosy fingers drew,

SOLITUDE.

Seldom shepherd's foot hath prest
One primrose in its sunny rest.
The sheep at distance from the spring
May here her lambkins chance to bring,
Sporting with their shadows airy,
Each like tiny Water-Fairy
Imaged in the lucid lake!
The hive-bee here doth sometimes make
Music, whose sweet murmurings tell,
Of his shelter'd straw-roof'd cell,
Standing 'mid some garden gay,
Near a cottage far away.
By the lake-side, on a stone
Stands the Heron all alone,
Still as any lifeless thing!
Slowly moves his laggard wing,
And cloud-like floating with the gale
Leaves at last the quiet vale.

BESSY BELL AND MARY GRAY.

[These orphans having attended the funeral of an aged woman with whom they had lived, retire from their native village, now desolated by the Plague, to a solitary glen. See the old Ballad that bears their names.]

THE grave is fill'd and the turf is spread
To grow together o'er the dead.
The little daisies bright and fair
Are looking up scarce injured there,
And one warm night of summer-dew
Will all their wonted smiles renew,
Restoring to its blooming rest
A soft couch for the sky-lark's breast.
The funeral-party, one by one
Have given their blessing and are gone—
Prepared themselves ere long to die,
A small, sad, silent company.
The orphans robed in spotless white

Yet linger in the holy ground,
And shed all o'er that peaceful mound
A radiance like the wan moonlight.
—Then from their mother's grave they glide
Out of the church-yard side by side.
Just at the gate they pause and turn—
I hear sad blended voices mourn
" Mother farewell!" the last endeavour
To send their souls back to the clay.
Then they hide their eyes—and walk away
From her grave—now and for ever!

Not till this parting invocation
To their mother's buried breast,
Had they felt the power of desolation!
Long as she lived, the village lay
Calm—unrepining in decay—
For grief was its own consolation,
And death seem'd only rest.
—But now a dim and sullen breath
Hath character'd the face of death;
And tears, and sighs, and sobs, and wailing,
All round—o'er human joy prevailing—
Or 'mid the pausing fits of woe,
Wild silence, like a depth of snow
Shrouding in slumber stern and dull
The spring-fields late so beautiful,
Upon their fainting spirits press

With weight of utter hopelessness,
And drive them off, they heed not where,
So that oblivion's ebbless wave
May lie for ever on one grave,
One village of despair.

Faint with such spectacles of woe
Towards their solitary home
Across the village-green they go—
Eyeing the streamlet's murmuring flow,
Where melt away the specks of foam,
Like human creatures dying
'Mid their voyage down life's peaceful stream !
Upon the bosom of a dream
In thoughtless pleasure lying.
Calm reveries of composing grief !
Whose very sadness yields relief
To heart, and soul, and eye.
The Orphans look around—and lo !
How touching is that Lilac's glow,
Beneath the tall Laburnum's bow
That dazzling spans the sky !
That golden gleam—that gentle fire
Forces even anguish to admire ;
And gently cheers away distress
By the power of nature's loveliness.
From many a little garden steal
Odours that have been wasting long

A sweetness there was none to feel ;
And from the hidden flowers a song
Of bees, in a happy multitude
All busy in that solitude,
An image brings of all the strife
And gladness of superior life,
Till man seem, 'mid these insects blest,
A brother-insect hardly miss'd.

They seize that transient calm ; the door
Of their own cottage open stands—
Far lonelier than one hour before,
When they with weak and trembling hands
The head of that dear coffin bore
Unto its darksome bed !
To them far drearier than the tomb,
The naked silence of the room
Deserted by the dead.
They kiss the dim and senseless walls,
Then hurry fast away ;
Some sudden thought their feet recals,
And trifles urge their stay,
Till with the violence of despair
They rush into the open air,
And bless its thatch and sheltering tree,
Then leave it everlastingly !
—On, on they go, in sorrow blind,
Yet with a still and gentle motion

That speaks the inner soul resign'd.
Like little billows o'er the ocean
Still flowing on with tide and wind,
And though the tempest smite their breast,
Reaching at last some bay of rest.

God bless them on their pilgrimage!
And may his hand divine
With healing dew their woes assuage,
When they have reach'd that silent shrine
By nature fram'd in the open air,
With soft turf for the knees of prayer,
And dome of many a pastoral hill
Lying in heaven serene and still.
For, pilgrims ne'er to Sion went
More mournful, or more innocent,
Before the rueful cross to lie
At midnight on Mount Calvary.

Two favourite sheep before them go—
Each with its lambs of spotless snow
Frisking around with pattering feet,
With peaceful eyes and happy bleat.
Happy! yet like a soft complaint!
As if at times the voice of sorrow
Through the hush'd air came breathing faint
From blessed things that fear no morrow.
—Each Shepherdess holds in her hand

A verdant crook of the willow-wand,
Wreath'd round with melancholy flowers
Gather'd 'mid the hills in happier hours.
In a small cage a thrush is sitting—
Or restless as the light
That through his sunny prison plays,
From perch to perch each moment flitting,
His quick and glancing eye surveys
The novel trees and fields so bright,
And like a torrent gushing strong
He sends through heaven his sudden song,
A song that all dim thought destroys,
And breathes o'er all its own wild joys.

As on the Orphans hold their way
Through the stillness of the dying day,
Fairies might they seem who are returning,
At the end of some allotted time,
Unto their own immortal clime!
Each bearing in its lovely hand
Some small memorial of the land
Where they, like common human frames,
And call'd by gentle Christian names,
For long had been sojourning!
Some little fair insensate thing,
Relic of that wild visiting!
Bird that beneath a brighter spring
Of its own vanish'd earth will sing;

Those harmless creatures that will glide
O'er faëry vales in earthly snow,
And from the faëry river's flow
Come forth more purely beautified.

Now with a wild and mournful song
The fair procession moves along,
While, by that tune so sweet
The little flock delighted, press
As if with human tenderness
Around the singer's feet.
Up—up the gentle slope they wind,
Leaving the laughing flowers behind
That seem to court their stay.
One moment on the top they stand,
At the wild-unfolding vale's command,
—Then down into that faëry land
Dream-like they sink away!

THE SCHOLAR'S FUNERAL.

Why hang the sweet bells mute in Magdalen-Tower,
Still wont to usher in delightful May,
The dewy silence of the morning hour
Cheering with many a changeful roundelay?
And those pure youthful voices where are they,
That hymning far up in the listening sky,
Seem'd issuing softly through the gates of day,
As if a troop of sainted souls on high
Were hovering o'er the earth with angel melody?

This day the pensive Choristers are mute,
The Tower stands silent in the shades of woe,
And well that darkness and those shadows suit
The solemn hush shed o'er the courts below.

On the First of May the Choristers ascend the beautiful Tower of Magdalen College, Oxford, and there sing a Latin hymn to the Season.

THE SCHOLAR'S FUNERAL.

There all is noiseless as a plain of snow,
Nor wandering footstep stirs the echoing wall.
Hark—hark! the muffled bell is tolling slow!
Into my mournful soul its warnings fall—
It is the solemn day of Vernon's funeral.

No sound last night was heard these courts within,
Save sleepless scholar sobbing in his cell;
For mirth had seem'd a sacrilegious sin
Against the dead whom all did love so well.
Only—at evening-prayer the holy swell
Of organ at the close of service sent
(While on their knees the awe-struck weepers fell,
Or on the pillar'd shade in anguish leant)
Through the dim echoing aisle a sorrowful lament.

All night the melancholy moonshine slept
O'er the lone chamber where his corpse was laid:
Amid the sighing groves the cold dews wept,
And the sad stars in glimmering beams array'd
In heaven seem'd mourning o'er the parted shade
Of him who knew the nature and the name
Of every orb to human ken display'd,
Whether on silent throne a steadfast flame,
Or roll'd in music round the Universal Frame.

And now the day looks mournful as the night,
For all o'er heaven black clouds begin to roll,

Through which the dim sun streams a fitful light
In sympathy with man's desponding soul.
Is nought around but images of dole!
The distant towers a kindred sorrow breathe,
Struck 'mid their own groves by that dismal toll;
And the grey cloisters, coldly stretch'd beneath,
Hush'd in profounder calm confess the power of death.

Sad for the glory that hath parted thence,
Through spire, tower, temple, theatre and dome
Mourns Oxford in her old magnificence,
Sublimely silent 'mid the sunless gloom.
But chief one College weeps her favourite's doom—
All hearts turn thither in the calm of morn;
Silent she standeth like one mighty tomb,
In reverend beauty—desolate—forlorn—
For her refulgent star is all-untimely shorn.

Her courts grow darker as the hour draws near
When that blest corpse must sink for evermore,
Let down by loving hands to dungeon drear
From the glad world of sunshine cover'd o'er
By the damp pavement of the silent floor!
—Sad all around—as when a gentle day
All dimly riseth o'er a wreck-strewn shore,
When Love at last hath ceas'd to heaven to pray,
And Grief hath wept her fill, and Hope turn'd sick away.

P

THE SCHOLAR'S FUNERAL.

Yea! even a careless stranger might perceive
That death and sorrow rule this doleful place—
Passing along the grey-hair'd menials grieve,
Nor is it hard a tender gloom to trace
On the young chorister's sunshiny face,
While slow returning from the mournful room
Of friend where they were weeping o'er the days
With Vernon past—profoundly sunk in gloom
The pale-fac'd scholar walks, still dreaming of the tomb.

Now ghastly sight and lowly-whispering sound
On every side the sadden'd spirit meet—
And notice give to all the courts around
Of doleful preparation—the rude feet
Of death's hir'd menials through this calm retreat
With careless tread are hurrying to and fro—
And loving hearts with pangs of anguish beat,
To see the cloisters blackening all below
With rueful sable plumes—a ghastly funeral-show.

—Come let us now with silent feet ascend
The stair that leads up to yon ancient tower—
—There, lieth in his shroud my dearest friend!
Oh! that the breath of sighs, the dewy shower
Stream'd from so many eye-lids had the power
Gently to stir, and raise up from its bed
The broken stalk of that consummate flower!
Nought may restore the odours once when shed,
That sunshine smiles in vain—it wakens not the dead!

Behold! his parents kneeling side by side,
Still as the body that is sleeping there!
Far off were they when their sweet Henry died,
At once they fell from bliss into despair.
What sorrows slumber in that silvery hair!
The old man groans, nor dares his face to show
To the glad day-light—while a sobbing prayer
Steals from the calmer partner of his woe,
Who gently lays her hand upon those locks of snow.

He lifts his eyes—quick through a parting cloud
The sun looks out—and fills the room with light,
Hath given a purer lustre to the shroud,
And plays and dances o'er those cheeks so white.
" Curst be the cruel Sun! who shines so bright
" Upon my dead boy's face! one kiss—one kiss—
" Before thou sink to everlasting night!
" My child—my child!—oh! how unlike to this
" The last embrace I gave in more than mortal bliss."

Pale as a statue bending o'er a tomb,
The childless mother! as a statue still!
But Resignation, Hope, and Faith illume
Her upward eyes! and her meek spirit fill
With downy peace, which blasts of earthly ill
May never ruffle more—a smile appears
At times to flit across her visage chill,
More awful rendering every gush of tears
Shed at the dark eclipse of all life's sunny years.

THE SCHOLAR'S FUNERAL.

The whole path from his cradle to his grave
She travels back with a bewilder'd brain!
Bright in the gales of youth his free locks wave,
As if their burnish'd beauty laugh'd at pain,
And god-like claim'd exemption from the reign
Of grief, decay, and death! Her touch doth meet
Lips cold as ice that ne'er will glow again,
And lo! from these wan lips unto his feet
Drawn by the hand of death a ghostly winding-sheet!

She hop'd to have seen him in yon hallow'd grove,
With gay companions laughing at his side,
And listening unto him whom all did love!
For she had heard with pure maternal pride
How science to his gaze unfolded wide
Her everlasting gates—but as he trod
The Temple's inner shrine, he sank and died—
And all of him that hath not gone to God
Within her loving clasp lies senseless as the clod.

With tottering steps she to the window goes.
Oh! what a glorious burst of light is there!
Rejoicing in his course the river flows,
And 'neath its coronet of dark-blue air
The stately Elm-grove rises fresh and fair,
Blest in the dewy silence of the skies!
She looks one moment—then in blind despair
Turns to the coffin where her Henry lies—
—The green earth laughs in vain before his closed eyes!

THE SCHOLAR'S FUNERAL.

The Old Man now hath no more tears to shed—
Wasted are all his groans so long and deep—
He looks as if he car'd not for the dead !
Or thought his Son would soon awake from sleep.
An agony there is that cannot weep,
That glares not on the visage, but is borne
Within the ruin'd spirits dungeon-keep,
In darkness and in silence most forlorn,
Hugging the grave-like gloom, nor wishing for the morn.

Lo ! suddenly he starteth from his knees !
And hurrying up and down, all round the walls
Glances wild looks—and now his pale hands seize,
Just as the light on its expression falls,
Yon picture, whose untroubled face recalls
A smile for ever banish'd from the air !
" O dark ! my Boy ! are now thy Father's halls !
" But I will hang this silent picture there,
" And morn and night will kneel before it in despair."

With trembling grasp he lifts the idle gown
Worn by his Son—then closing his dim eyes,
With a convulsive start he flings it down,
Goes and returns, and loads it where it lies
With hurried kisses ! Then his glance espies
A letter by that hand now icy-cold
Fill'd full of love, and homebred sympathies ;
Naming familiarly both young and old,
And blessing that sweet Home he ne'er was to behold.

THE SCHOLAR'S FUNERAL.

And now the Father lays his wither'd hand
Upon a book whose leaves are idly spread:
Gone—gone is he who well could understand
The kingly language of the mighty dead!
—There lies the flute that oft at twilight shed
Airs that beguil'd the old man of his tears;
But cold the master's touch—his skill is fled,
And all his innocent life at once appears
Like some sweet lovely tune that charm'd in other years.

But now the door is open'd soft and slow,
" The hour is come, and all the mourners wait
" With heads uncover'd in the courts below!"
Stunn'd are the parents with these words of fate,
And bow their heads low down beneath the weight
Of one soul-sickening moment of despair!
Grief cometh deadly when it cometh late,
And with a Fury's hand delights to tear
From Eld's deep-furrow'd front the thin and hoary hair.

His eyes are open, and with tearless gleam
Fix'd on the coffin! but they see it not,
Like haunted Guilt blind-walking in a dream,
With soul intent on its own secret blot.
The coffin moves!—yet rooted to the spot,
He sees it borne away, with vacant eyes,
Unconscious what it means! hath even forgot
The name of Her who in a death-fit lies,—
His heart is turn'd to stone, nor heeds who lives or dies!

THE SCHOLAR'S FUNERAL.

Lo! now the Pall comes forth into the light
And one chill shudder thrills the weeping crowd!
There is it 'mid the sunshine black as night!
And soon to disappear—a passing cloud!
Grief can no longer bear—but bursts aloud!
Youth, manhood, age, one common nature sways
And hoary heads across the pall are bowed
Near burnish'd locks where youthful beauty plays—
For all alike did love the Form that there decays!

List! list! a doleful dirge—a wild death-song!
The coffin now is placed upon its bier,
And through the echoing cloisters borne along!
—How touching those young voices thus to hear
Singing of sorrow, and of mortal fear
To their glad innocence as yet unknown!
Singing they weep—but transient every tear,
Nor may their spirits understand the groan
That age or manhood pours above the funeral stone.

Waileth more dolefully that passing psalm,
At every step they take towards the cell
That calls the coffin to eternal calm!
At each swing of the melancholy bell
More loud the sighing and the sobbing swell,
More ghostly paleness whitens every face!
Slow the procession moves—slow tolls that knell—
But yet the funeral at that solemn pace
Alas! too soon will reach its final resting-place.

THE SCHOLAR'S FUNERAL.

How Vernon lov'd to walk this cloister'd shade
In silent musings, far into the night!
When o'er that Tower the rising Moon display'd
Not purer than his soul her cloudless light.
Still was his lamp-lit window burning bright,
A little earthly star that shone most sweet
To those in heaven—but now extinguish'd quite—
—Fast-chain'd are now those nightly-wand'ring feet
In bonds that none may burst—folds of the winding-sheet.

Wide is the chapel-gate, and entereth slow
With all its floating pomp that sable pall!
Silent as in a dream the funeral show
(For grief hath breath'd one spirit into all)
Is ranged at once along the gloomy wall!
Ah me! what mournful lights athwart the gloom,
From yonder richly-pictur'd window fall!
And with a transitory smile illume
The dim-discover'd depth of that damp breathless tomb.

All hearts turn shuddering from that gulf profound,
And momentary solace vainly seek
In gazing on the solemn objects round!
Those pictur'd saints with eyes uplifted meek
To the still heavens, how silently they speak
Of faith untroubled, sanctity divine—
While on the paleness of each placid cheek
We seem to see a holy lustre shine
O'er mortal beauty breath'd from an immortal shrine!

THE SCHOLAR'S FUNERAL.

What though beneath our feet the earthly mould
Of virtue, beauty, youth, and genius lie
In grim decay ! Yet round us we behold
The cheering emblems of eternity.
What voice divine is theirs ! If soul may die,
And nought its perishable glory save,
Unto yon marble face that to the sky
Looks up with humble hope, what feeling gave
Those smiles that speak of heaven, though kindling o'er
      a grave !

O holy image of the Son of God !
Bearing his cross up toilsome Calvary !
Was that stern path for sinful mortals trod ?
—Methinks from that calm cheek, and pitying eye
Uplifted to that grim and wrathful sky,
(Dim for our sakes with a celestial tear)
Falls a sweet smile where Vernon's relics lie
In mortal stillness on the unmoving bier !
Seeming the bright spring-morn of heaven's eternal year.

—Down, down within oblivion's darksome brink
With lingering motion, as if every hand
Were loth to let the mournful burden sink,
The coffin disappears ! The weeping band,
All round that gulf one little moment stand
In mute and blank dismay—and scarcely know
What dire event has happen'd ! the loose sand
From the vault-stone with dull drop sounds below,—
The grave's low hollow voice hath told the tale of woe !

THE SCHOLAR'S FUNERAL.

Look for the last time down that cold damp gloom;
Of those bright letters take a farewel sight!
—Down falls the vault-stone on the yawning tomb,
And all below is sunk in sudden night!
Now is the chapel-aisle with sunshine bright,
The upper world is glad, and fresh and fair,
But that black stone repels the dancing light,—
The beams of heaven must never enter there,
Where by the mould'ring corpse in darkness sits Despair!

Where now those tears, smiles, motions, looks and tones,
That made our Vernon in his pride of place
So glorious and so fair! these sullen stones,
Like a frozen sea, lie o'er that beauteous face!
Soon will there be no solitary trace
Of him, his joys, his sadness, or his mirth!
Even now grows dim the memory of that grace
That halo-like shone round the soul of worth!
All fading like a dream! all vanishing from earth.

Where now the fancies wild—the thoughts benign
That rais'd his soul and purified his heart!
Where now have fled those impulses divine
That taught that gifted youth the Poet's art,
Stealing at midnight with a thrilling start
Into his spirit, wakeful with the pain
Of that mysterious joy! In darkness part
All the bright hopes, that in a glorious train
Lay round his soul, like clouds that hail the morning's
  reign!

THE SCHOLAR'S FUNERAL.

Ah me! can sorrow such fair image bring
Before a mourner's eyes! Methinks I see,
Laden with all the glories of the spring,
Balm, brightness, music, a resplendent tree,
Waving its blossom'd branches gloriously
Over a sunny garden of delight!
A cold north-wind comes wrathful from the sea,
And there at dawn of day a rueful sight!
As winter brown and sere, the glory once so bright.

I look into the mist of future years,
And gather comfort from the eternal law
That yields up manhood to a host of fears,
To blinded passion, and bewildering awe!
Th' exulting soul of Vernon never saw
Hope's ghastly visage by Truth laugh'd to scorn;
Imagination had not paus'd to draw
The gorgeous curtains of Life's sunny morn,
Nor show'd the scenes behind so dismal and forlorn.

To thee, my Friend! as to a shining star
Through the blue depths a cloudless course was given;
There smil'd thy soul, from earthly vapours far,
Serenely sparkling in its native heaven!
No clouds at last were o'er its beauty driven—
But as aloft it burn'd resplendently,
At once it faded from the face of even,
As oft before the nightly wanderer's eye
A star on which he gaz'd drops sudden from the sky!

Who comes to break my dreams? The chapel-door
Is opening slow, and that old Man appears
With his long floating locks so silvery-hoar!
His frame is crouching, as if twenty years
Had pass'd in one short day! There are no tears
On his wan wrinkled face, or hollow eyes!
At last with pain his humbled head he rears,
And asks, while not one grief-chok'd voice replies,
" Show me the very stone 'neath which my Henry
    lies!"

He sees the scatter'd dust—and down he falls
Upon that pavement with a shuddering groan—
And with a faultering broken voice he calls
By that dear name upon his buried Son.
Then dumb he lies! and ever and anon
Fixes his eye-balls with a ghastly glow
On the damp blackness of that hideous stone,
As if he look'd it through, and saw below
The dead face looking up as white as frozen snow!

O gently make way for that Lady fair!
How calm she walks along the solemn aisle!
Beneath the sad grace of that braided hair,
How still her brow! and what a holy smile!
One start she gives—and stops a little while,
When bow'd by grief her husband's frame appears,
With reverend locks which the hard stones defile!

THE SCHOLAR'S FUNERAL.

Then with the only voice that mourner hears,
Lifts up his hoary head and bathes it in her tears!

At last the funeral party melts away,
And as I look up from the chapel-floor,
No living object can my eyes survey,
Save these two childless Parents at the door,
Flinging back a wild farewell—then seen no more!
And now I hear my own slow footsteps sound
Along the echoing aisle—that tread is o'er—
And as with blinded eyes I turn me round,
The Sexton shuts the gate that stuns with thundering
　　sound!

How fresh and cheerful laughs the open air
To one who has been standing by a tomb!
And yet the beauty that is glistening there
Flings back th' unwilling soul into the gloom.
We turn from walls which dancing rays illume
Unto the darkness where we lately stood,
And still the image of that narrow room
Beneath the sunshine chills our very blood,
With the damp breathless air of mortal solitude.

O band of rosy children shouting loud,
With morris-dance in honour of the May!
Restrain that laughter ye delighted crowd,
Let one sad hour disturb your holiday.

Ye drop your flowers, and wonder who are they
With garb so black and cheeks of deadly hue!
With one consent then rush again to play,
For what hath Sadness, Sorrow, Death to do,
Beneath that sunny sky with that light-hearted crew!

And now the Parents have left far behind
The gorgeous City with its groves and bowers,
The funeral toll pursues them on the wind,
And looking back, a cloud of thunder lowers
In mortal darkness o'er the shining towers,
That glance like fire at every sunny gleam!
Within that glorious scene, what hideous hours
Dragg'd their dire length! tower, palace, temple swim,
Before their wilder'd brain—a grand but dreadful
    dream!

Say who will greet them at their Castle-gate?
A silent line in sable garb array'd,
The ancient servants of the House will wait!
Up to those woe-worn visages afraid
To lift their gaze! while on the Tower displayed,
A rueful scutcheon meets the Father's eye,
Hung out by death when beauty had decayed,
And sending far into the sunless sky
The mortal gloom that shrouds its dark emblazonry.

THE SCHOLAR'S FUNERAL.

Oh! black as death yon pine-grove on the hill!
Yon waterfall hath now a dismal roar!
Why is that little lake so sadly still,
So dim the flowers and trees along the shore!
'Tis not in vernal sunshine to restore
Their faded beauty, for the source of light
That warm'd the primrose-bank doth flow no more!
Vain Nature's power! for unto Sorrow's sight
No dewy flower is fair, no blossomy tree is bright.

—Five years have travell'd by—since side by side
That aged pair were laid in holy ground!
With them the very name of Vernon died,
And now it seemeth like an alien sound,
Where once it shed bright smiles and blessings round!
Another race dwell in that ancient Hall,
Nor one memorial of that youth is found
Save his sweet Picture—now unknown to all—
That smiles, and long will smile neglected on the wall.

But not forgotten in that lofty clime,
Where star-like once thy radiant spirit shone,
Art thou my Vernon! 'mid those courts sublime
The mournful music of thy name is known.
Oxford still glories in her gifted Son,
And grey-hair'd men who speak of days gone by
Recount what noble palms by him were won,
Describe his step, his mien, his voice, his eye,
Till tears will oft rush in to close his eulogy.

THE SCHOLAR'S FUNERAL.

In the dim silence of the Chapel-aisle
His Image stands! with pale but life-like face!
The cold white marble breathes a heavenly smile,
The still locks cluster with a mournful grace.
O ne'er may time that beauteous bust deface!
There may it smile through ages far away,
On those, who, walking through that holy place,
A moment pause that Image to survey,
And read with soften'd soul the monumental lay.

THE CONVICT.

PART I.

SCENE I.

A room in a cottage at Lea-side.—The Prisoner's Wife, and a Friend sitting together in the midst of the Family.—The day on which sentence was to be pronounced.

Wife. 'Tis twelve o'clock, and no news from the City.
Oh! had he been acquitted, many hundreds
Would have been hurried hither in their joy,
Headlong into the house of misery,
To shout the tidings of salvation there.
But now that he is doom'd unto the death,
They fear to bring with black and silent faces
The sentence of despair. O God! to think
That all this long interminable night,
Which I have pass'd in thinking on two words—
"Guilty"—"not guilty!" like one happy moment,
O'er many a head hath flown unheeded by—
O'er happy sleepers dreaming in their bliss

Of bright to-morrows—or far happier still
With deep breath buried in forgetfulness.
O all the dismallest images of death
Did swim before my eyes! The cruel face
Of that most wicked old man, whom in youth
I once saw in the City—that wan wretch
The public Executioner, rose up
Close by my husband's side, and in his hand
A most accursed halter, which he shook
In savage mockery—and then grimly smiled,
Pointing to a scaffold with his shrivell'd fingers,
Where, on a sudden, my own husband stood
Drest all in white, and with a fixed face
Far whiter still—I felt as if in hell,
And shrieked out till my weeping children rose
In terror from their beds.

  Friend.   'Twas but a dream.

  Wife. No, I was broad awake—but still the vision
Stood steadfastly before me—till I sank
Upon my knees in prayer—and Jesus Christ
Had pity on me—and it came no more.

  Friend. Full many a sleepless eye did weep for thee
Last night, and for thy husband. Think it not
That pity dwells not in the hearts of kindred.
Even strangers weep—they think him innocent,
And prayers from many who never saw his face,
For him have gone to heaven—they will be heard.

Wife. Oh! what are prayers, and shriekings of despair,
Or frantic outcries of insanity,
Unto the ear of the great dreadful God!
Can we believe that prayers of ours will change
Th' Almighty's steadfast purpose! Things like us!
Poor miserable worms!—All night I cried
" Save, save my husband God! O save my husband!"
But back the words return'd unto my heart,
And the dead silence of the senseless walls
With horrid mockery in the darkness stood
Between me and my God.
 Friend.   Yet it is written,
" Ask and it shall be given thee."
 Wife.   Blessed words!
And did they come from his most holy lips
Who cannot lie?
 Friend.   They are our Saviour's words.
 Wife. Joy, joy unto the wretched! Hear me then,
O Son of God! while near my cradled infant
Sleeping in ignorance of its Father's sorrows,
I fall down on my knees before thy face!
Hear, hear the broken voice of misery!
" Ask and it shall be given thee!" Holy One!
I ask, beseech, implore, and supplicate,
That Thou wilt save my husband, and henceforth
Will I an alter'd creature walk this earth

With Thee, and none but Thee, most Holy Being,
For ever in my heart, my inmost heart.
 Friend. Is not my friend already comforted?
 Wife. The heavy burden of despair is lighten'd.
In this my hour of tribulation
My Saviour's words return upon my heart,
Like breath of Spring reviving the dead flowers
In our sweet little garden.
 Friend.   Heaven bless thee,
A smile is on thy cheek, a languid smile!
 Wife. I know not why I smiled—a sudden gleam
Of hope did flash across me.—Hark! a footstep!
 Friend. 'Tis the dog stirring on his straw.
 Wife.   Poor Luath!
Thy kind affectionate heart doth miss thy master.
Mary! the poor dumb creature walks about
As if some sickness wore him, always wandering
Round, round the house, and all the neighbouring fields,
Seeking the absent. He will disappear
For hours together, and come home at night
Wearied and joyless—for he has been running
No doubt o'er all the hills, and round the lochs,
Trying to find his master's well-known footsteps.
Then will he look with dim complaining eyes
Full in my face, and with a wailing whine
Goes to his straw, and there at once lies down
Without a gambol or a loving frisk
Among the little children. Many a Christian

Might take a lesson from that poor dumb creature.
—When Frank comes home—how Luath will partake
The general happiness! When Frank comes home!
What am I raving of? When Frank comes home!
That blank and weeping face too plainly says
" That hour will never be!" Look not so black,
Unless you wish to kill me with despair.

Friend. I wished not to appear so sorrowful.
Within the silent grave my husband sleeps,
And I am reconciled unto the doom
Of widowhood—this Babe doth reconcile me.
But thine is lying in the fearful darkness
Of an uncertain fate—and I now feel
A beating at my heart—a cold sick flutter
That sends this black expression to my face,
Although it nothing mean.

Wife. O that some bird,
Some beautiful bird with soft and purple feathers,
Would sail into this room, in silence floating
All round these blessed walls, with the boon of life
Beneath its outspread wings—a holy letter
In mercy written by an angel's hand,
In bright words speaking of deliverance!
—A raven! hear that dismal raven croak
Of death and judgment! See the Demon sitting
On the green before the window—croak, croak, croak!
'Tis the Evil-One in likeness of that bird
Enjoying there my mortal misery!

Boy. 'Tis not a raven mother—the tame crow
Of cousin William, that comes hopping here
With its clipt wings—aye, almost every day—
My father himself oft fed that bird, and put it
Upon my head, where it would sit and caw,
And flutter with its wings,—and all the while
My father laugh'd—it was so comical
He said, to see that black and sooty crow
Sitting on my white hair.
 Wife.   Your father laugh'd!
     [*Laughing herself hysterically.*]
 Boy. Oh! that he were come back from prison—
  Mother!
Last night I fought a boy who said in sport
That my father would be hanged.
 Wife.   The little wretch!
What did he say?
 Boy.   That my father would be hanged!
 Wife. O God! the senseless child did speak the truth!
He hath heard his parents talking of the trial,
And in his careless levity repeated
The shocking words—aye—laughing all the while,
Then running to his play—perhaps intending
To ask the master for a holiday
To see the execution. Cursed brat!
What place is sacred held from cruelty,
When it doth leer within an infant's eyes
And harden his glad heart!

Boy.   I beat him mother.
He is a lying boy—he ne'er speaks truth—
And when my father is come home again,
I will ask him if he recollects that saying!
No, I will look at him, and pass him by
With a proud smiling face—I will forgive him
And shake hands with him in my happiness.
   Wife. The sun is shining—children go to play
For an hour out-of-doors.
   Boy.   Come—sisters, come!
We will go out-of-doors—but not to play.
Come to the little green-plat in the wood,
And say our prayers together for our father.
Then if we play—'twill be some gentle game,
And all the while we will think upon our father
Coming out of that dark cell.—Come sisters—come!
   Friend. Children so good as these must not be or-
         phans!
Yet I am glad to see thy soul prepar'd
Even for the worst.
   Wife.   My soul prepared for the worst!
No! that can never be—*(goes to the window.)*—A cloud
         of thunder
Is hanging o'er the city! black as night!
I hear it rumbling—what a hollow growl!
O dreadful building where the Judge is sitting
In judgment on my husband! All the darkness
Of the disturbed heavens is on its walls.

—And now the fatal sentence is pronouncing.
The Court at once is hush'd—and every eye
Bent on my husband! " Hanged till you are dead,
" Hanged by the neck!"—As thou dost hope for mercy,
O savage Judge! recal these wicked words!
For thy own wife who waits for thee at home
Is not more innocent than my poor husband!

[*She flings herself down on the floor in an agony of grief.*]

Friend. Mercy is with the King—and he is merciful!
Wife. What! what! do you believe an innocent man
Was e'er condemned to die!—To die for murder!
—Did mercy ever reach one so condemn'd?
Friend. Yes! I have read of one wretch pardoned
Even on the scaffold—where the light of truth
Struck, like the sunshine suddenly burst forth,
And tinged with fearful joy the ghastly face
Of him who had no thought but that of death.
And back unto his widow-wife went he,
Like a ghost from the grave—and there he sat
Before the eyes of her who knew him not,
But took him for a vision, and fell down
In a death-fit of wilder'd happiness.
Wife. Mercy dwells with the King—and he is merciful.
O blest for ever be the hoary head
Of our kind-hearted King!—I will away
And fling myself down before his royal feet!
Who knows but that the monarch in his palace

Will see within his soul this wretched cottage,
And, like a saving angel, with one word
Breathe over it the air of paradise.
—Mercy is with the King—and he is merciful.

Friend. Fortune is blind—but justice eagle-eyed,
He will not be condemned.

Wife. Give me some water!
My soul is faint with thirst!—Do they not say
That men upon the scaffold call for water?
—" Give me a glass of water!" 'tis his voice—
My husband's voice!—No! he is not condemned!
A thousand voices from these silent walls
Cry out " he shall not die!"—

Enter a young CLERGYMAN.

Clergyman. Methinks that God hath shed a calm to-day
Over the house of mourning. Is it so?

Wife. Thy presence brings a calm. Oh! one like thee
Should bear good tidings.

Clergyman. Last night in his cell
I saw your husband after his long trial,
And sure I am that never did he sit
Even in this room among his family
With more composed face, or stiller soul,
Than he sat there upon his bed of straw,
With fetters on his limbs.

Wife.   Fetters on his limbs!
Clergyman. He felt them not—or if he faintly felt
    them,
It was not in his soul—for it was free
As a lark in heaven.
    Wife.   He was not shedding tears!
Clergyman. No—with a calm and quiet face he look'd
    at me,
And in his eyes there was a steadfast light
By grief unclouded, and undimm'd by tears.
So was it while the blameless man was speaking
Of himself and of his trial: then he spake
Of those he loved, and as he breath'd the name
Of this sweet farm " Lea-side !" then truly tears
Did force their way, but soon he wip'd them off,
And rais'd to heaven a clear unfaltering prayer
For his wife and children—the most touching prayer,
I think, that ever flowed from human lips!
  Wife. Is there no hope, then, after all, of life!
  Clergyman. Yes! there is hope—though I am forc'd
    to say
That he doth stand upon the darksome brink
Of danger and of death.
    Wife.   I hear thy words,
And I can bear them! For my suffering spirit
Hath undergone its pains, and I am left,
Even like a woman after travail, weak—

But in a slumbrous quiet that succeeds
The hour of agony.   [*She sinks into sleep.*]
   Clergyman. My friend! behold
How quietly that worn-out wretch doth sleep.
   Friend. Calm as an infant!
   Clergyman.   Even too deep for dreams!
How meekly beautiful her face doth smile
As from a soul that never had known grief.
Methinks that God, in that profound repose,
Will breathe submission through her innocent soul,
And she who lay down with a mortal's weakness
May wake in power and glory like an angel
Whom trouble cannot touch.

Enter the Children weeping.

   Friend. What ails ye my sweet children—but speak
      softly—
Your mother is asleep.
   Girl.   O tell it, brother!
For my heart beats so that I cannot speak!
   Boy. When we were coming homewards down the
      lane
That leads from the Fox-wood, that old dumb Woman
Who tells folk's fortunes, from behind the hedge
Leapt out upon the road, before our faces,
And with that dreadful barking voice of hers,
And grinning mouth, and red and fiery eyes,
All the while shaking at us her black hair,

She took a rope of rushes and did tie it
Like a halter round her neck, and pull'd it tight
Till she grew black in the face! Then shook her hand
Against our cottage, while my father's name
Seem'd half-pronounc'd in that most hideous gabble.
Then with one spring she leapt behind the hedge,
Where, as we ran away, we heard her laughing!
And oh! a long, loud, cruel laugh it was!
As if she laugh'd to know that our poor father
Was now condemned to die!

Friend. O wicked wretch! the silence of her soul
Is fill'd with cruel thoughts—even like a mad-house
With the din of creatures raving. None can guess
The wrath of this dumb savage!

> [*The door opens, and the dumb woman enters making a hideous noise, and with signs intimating that some one is to be hanged. The prisoner's wife, wakened by the noise, starts from her sleep.*]

Wife. Thou silent, speechless messenger of death!
Louder thy dumbness than a roaring cannon!
Away—away—thou fury from my sight.
—God save me from that woman! or deliver
Her soul from the devils that torment her thus.

> [*The children hide themselves, and the dumb woman rushes out with peals of wild laughter.*]

Her face was black with death—a hellish joy
Shone through her idiot eyes—as if a fiend
Had taken that rueful body for a dwelling,

And from these glazed sockets lov'd to look
With a horrid leer upon us mortal creatures,
A leer of unrepentant wickedness,
Hating us because we are the work of God!

  Boy. I wish that she were dead and buried.

  Wife. O now that she is gone, hope leaps again
Within my heart—her hideous mummery
Must not be suffer'd to confound me so.
And yet, they say, that she did prophecy,
With the wild motions of her witch-like hands,
That fatal sinking of the ferry-boat
In which whole families perished. Hush! I hear
The tread of feet—it is the Messenger
Come from the City.

  [*Enter* MESSENGER *with a letter in his hand.*]

  Wife.   Speak, speak instantly—
Speak! Why do you come here unless you speak?
—His face doth seem composed.

  Messenger.   Poor Francis Russel!
Now all is over with him—he is condemned!

  Wife. What did he say?—Why art thou gabbling
    thus,
As none can understand?—Give me that letter.
          [*Tears it open and reads it aloud.*]
" They have found me guilty, Mary! trust in God."
    [*She flings herself down on the floor, and her Child-*
    ren lie down crying beside her.]

Messenger. I cannot bear the sight—good folks, farewell.

Wife. "My Mary trust in God." I cannot trust
In God!—Oh! wilt thou in thy wrath allow
My innocent husband thus to be destroyed?——
I cannot trust in God! O cursed for ever
Be all the swarm of idiot witnesses,
Jury and Judge, who thus have murder'd him,
And may his blood for generations lie
Heavy on their children's souls!

Girl. O brother! see
'Tis our poor Father's writing. Yet his hand
Seems never to have shaken.—Innocence,
He used to say, did make small children fearless,
And it will make him happy in his prison,
Till we rush in, and wait till he is pardon'd,
Which will be·········

Wife. Never will he leave his dungeon
But for the scaffold. Would that I were dead,
And all my children corpses at my side,
Never again to wake······for Mercy is not
In heaven or earth. There is no Providence!
  [*Covers her face, and tears her hair.*]

Clergyman. These are affecting words from one so good
And truly pious. But our human nature,
When touch'd at the heart by Misery's icy hand,
Oft shrieks out with a wild impiety,

Against its better will.   Yet that shrill cry
Is heard in heaven with pity, and on earth
Is often followed by the calm still voice
Of resignation melting into prayer.

Wife, (starting up). Where art thou? What impe-
                netrable cloud
Hides thee from justice, thou grim murderer!
On whom the dead man's blood, the quick man's tears,
Now call with twofold vengeance? Drive him forth,
O Fear! into the light, and I shall know him,
Soon as my eye meets his.   His very name
Will burst instinctively from my big heart,
And he will answer to it.   Where art thou
With thy red hands, that never may be cleans'd?

Friend. 'Tis five weeks to the day of execution,
And he may be discover'd—

Wife.   Execution!
And will they make my husband mount a ladder
Up to a scaffold! May he rather die
Of anguish in his cell!—Where are my children?
—O they are weeping even upon my breast!
—Would they had ne'er been born!—Eternal shame
Will lie upon them! lovely as they are,
And good, and pure, and innocent as angels,
They will be scorn'd and hated!—Save my husband,
Great God of Mercy! Jesus! save my husband.
—O many thousand miles of clouds and air
Lie between me and God! and my faint voice

Returns unto the earth, while the still heavens,
Like the deep sea above a drowning head,
Mind not the stifled groans of agony!

Clergyman. I will go to his cell and pray with him.
He had foreseen his doom,—and be assured
That he is sitting in the eye of God,
With meek composure, not in agony.

The Children. O take us with you.

Clergyman.   For a while farewell,
The wife's heart now is like a heavy cloud!
But tears will lighten it—God be with you all!

SCENE II.

The condemned Cell.—The Prisoner *in Chains.—The Prison clock strikes.*

Prisoner. That was a dreadful toll! it brings me nearer
Unto the day of horror. Here am I
Deliver'd over to the fear of death
In cold and rueful solitude—shut out
By that black vault of stone from memory
Of human beings—and, as it would seem,
From the pity of my God! Who thinks on me?
The crowd that came to hear my sentence past
Are scatter'd o'er the City, and my fate
Is by them all forgotten, or pronounced
With faces of indifference or of pleasure,

Among the chance discoursing of the day.
And yet my silent solitary cell
Is in the heart of life!—O joyful sound
Of life and freedom in a rushing tumult
Sweeping o'er the streets in the bright open day!
O that I were a beggar cloth'd in rags!
Prey'd on by cold and hunger—and with wounds
Incurable, worn down unto a shadow,
So that I knew not when I was to die!
—I hear the blind man singing in the street
With a clear gladsome voice, a jocund song!
What is the loss of eyes!—Thou bawling wretch
Disturb him not! With what a hideous twang
He howls out to the passing traveller,
" A full account of Francis Russel's trial,
" The murderer's confession."——Save my soul—
O save me from that hideous skeleton!....

[*Dashes himself on the floor.*]

The JAILOR *enters with bread and water.*

Jailor. Look up my friend—I bring you some refreshment.

Prisoner. (*Staring wildly.*) Art thou the executioner?
Jailor.   No. The Jailor.
Prisoner. Is the fatal hour arrived?
Jailor.   I'm not the hangman.
Prisoner. One single drop of wine! These two last days

Have put my blood into a burning fever,
Yet the thought of water sickens at my heart.
One single drop of wine.

   Jailor.   I must not give it.

   Prisoner. O that a want like this should seem a hard-
      ship
To one condemned to die! My wretched body
With fiery fever wastes my quaking soul,
And rather would I have one drop of wine
Than voice of friends or prayers of holy men,
So faint and thirsty is my very being.

   Jailor. What must be must.

   Prisoner.   O cold and heavy chains!
How shockingly they glitter as they clank!

   Jailor. You soon will get accustom'd to their weight.
Observe that ring there runs along the staunchel,
On the stone-floor—so you may drag your legs
From wall to wall with little difficulty,
And in a week or two you'll never heed
The clanking of the iron. The last criminal
Was but a lath of a man compared with you,
And yet whene'er I came into his cell
I found him always merrily at work,
Back back and forward whisking constantly
Like a bird in his cage.

   Prisoner.   Was he set free at last?

   Jailor. Aye. Jack Ketch set him free.

   Prisoner.   What was his crime?

Jailor. A murderer like yourself. He kill'd his sweet-
    heart,
And threw her, though some six months gone with child,
Into a coal-pit.
Prisoner. (*sternly.*) Leave me to myself.
Jailor. Why! Man, I wish to be on good terms with
    you.
I am your friend. What! many a noble fellow
Hath in his day done murder: in the name
There may be something awkward—but the act
Still varies with the change of circumstance—
I would as lief shake hands with thee my friend
As with the Judge himself.
Prisoner. (*eagerly.*)   Dost think me innocent?
Jailor. (*ironically.*) O yes! as innocent as any lamb.
But hark ye! if that I allow your friends
To visit you at times, you in return
Will let me shew you to the country-people
On a chance market-day.
Prisoner.   O God of mercy!
Jailor. There will they stand beyond reach of your
    arm,
With open mouth and eyes like idiots.
Then look unto each other—shake their heads
And crying out, " God bless us!" leave the cell,
No doubt much wiser than they came—quite proud
To think how they will make their neighbours shudder
At the picture of thy murderous countenance,

And eyes so like a demon's—we will share
The money, friend‥‥
   Prisoner.   The money!—What of money?
   Jailor. Why you are surely deaf‥‥‥
   Prisoner.   Give me the water.
                              [*Drinks eagerly.*]
Take—take the bread that I may die of hunger.
           [*The* JAILOR *goes out of the cell.*]
I feel as if buried many a fathom deep
In a cave below the sea, or in some pit
Cover'd o'er with thorns amid a darksome wood,
Where one might lie from Sabbath unto Sabbath
Shrieking madly out for help, but all in vain,
Unto the solitary trees, or clouds
That past unheeding o'er the far-off heavens!
Five weeks must drag their days and nights along
Through the damp silence of this lonesome cell,
And all that time must I be sitting here
In doleful dreams—or lying on this straw
With nought but shivering terror in my soul—
Or hurrying up and down with clanking chains
In wrath and sickness and insanity,
A furious madman preying on myself
And dash'd against the walls. What spirit moves
These bolts? O welcome whosoe'er thou art!
A very demon's presence in this dungeon
Would be a comfort.
    [*The door opens, and the young* CLERGYMAN *enters.*]

Son of righteousness!
Let me fall down in worship at thy feet.
 Clergyman. O man of trouble! put your trust in God.
Morning and evening will I seek your cell
And read the Bible with you. Rise—O rise!
 Prisoner. Despise me not that on this cruel pavement
I dash myself down in fear and agony,
And grovel at your feet! A pitiful wretch
Indeed am I; and to preserve my life
Would hang my head in everlasting shame,
Or a lonesome hunger'd in a desert dwell
Doom'd never more to sleep.
 Clergyman.   Unhappy man!
Say what thou wilt, for I will listen to thee.
 Prisoner (looking up.) Can you not save me?—On a
            quiet bed,
Surrounded by my weeping family,
I might have died like other mortal creatures
In awful resignation; but to stand
Upon a scaffold in my native parish,
With a base halter round my abject neck,
Stared at, and hiss'd at, shudder'd at, and scorn'd,
Put out of life, like a dog, with every insult
Cruelly forced on my immortal soul,
And then····O Christ, I hear a skeleton
Rattling in chains!—To a madhouse carry me,
Bind me to the floor, that when the day arrives
The hangman's hand may strive in vain to burst
The bolts that chain the Lunatic to life.

I will feign madness.   No—Eternal God !
I need not feign, for like a tide it cometh,
Wave after wave, upon my choking spirit....
I am bound to a stake within the mark o' the sea,
And the cold drowning mounts up from my feet.
   Clergyman. Send peace, O Lord! unto the sufferer's
      heart.
   Prisoner. Suddenly, suddenly in my happiness
The curse did smite me.   O my gentle Alice,
Is the sweet baby now upon thy breast ?
The Mother and the Infant both will die.
The dreadful day of execution
Will murder us all, and Lea-side then will be
Silent as the grave.   O fearful Providence,
Darken my brain, that I may think no more
On thy wild ways that only lead to death,
To misery, to madness, and to hell !
Is all I say not true ? Didst hear him speak ?
That savage Judge, who with a hollow voice,
As if he had a pleasure in my anguish,
Continued speaking hours most bitterly
Against a quaking prisoner bow'd with shame ?
He had forgotten that I was a Man !
And ever as he turn'd his harden'd eye
Towards the bar, it froze my very heart ;
So proud, so cruel, and so full of scorn.
I think he might have wept, for many wept
When he pass'd sentence on me—but his voice

Was calm and steady, and his eye was clear,
Looking untroubled on the face of trouble.
I did not faint—No—though a sickening pang
Tugg'd at my heart, and made the cold sweat creep
Like ice-drops o'er my body—yet even then
Did conscious innocence uphold my soul,
And turn'd the horrid words to senseless sounds
That ought not to dismay—while he that sat
In pompous robes upon the judgment-seat,
Seem'd in his blind unfeeling ignorance
A verier wretch than I.

Clergyman.   We all are blind,
And duty's brow is stern, and harsh his voice.
That Judge is famed for his humanity,
And though no tears were in his solemn eyes,
They flow'd within his heart.

Prisoner.   I do forgive him.
What shrieks were these?

Clergyman.   Of a poor criminal
In the next cell.

Prisoner.   Condemn'd like me to die!

Clergyman. No! doom'd to drag out in a foreign
        land,
Unpitied years of misery and shame.

Prisoner. O happy lot! who would not leap with joy
Into the ship that bore him to the land
Of shame and toil, and crime and wickedness,
So that with all his load of misery

He might escape from death! May not I escape?
Bolts have been riven, and walls been undermin'd,
And the free winds have borne the prisoner
To the dark depths of safety—never more
To walk the streets of cities, but to dwell
As in the shadow of the grave, unknown
But to his own soul silent as the night!
I feel a wild hope springing from despair!
That shadow was not mine that stood all-white
Shivering on a scaffold:—Sampson's strength is here,
And the hard stone to my unwearied hand
Will crumble into dust.

   Clergyman.   O let us pray!

   Prisoner. Yes, I will pray! pray for deliverance,
And years to come! O be they what they may,
For life is sweet, embitter'd though it be
With the lowest dregs in the cup of misery!

   Clergyman. Shall we kneel down?

   Prisoner.   Aye! they will dance and dance,
And smile and laugh, and talk of pleasant things,
And listen to sweet music all the night,
That I am lying fetter'd to the straw
In dire convulsions. They will speak of me
Amid their mirth and music, but will see not
My image in their souls, or it would strike them
With palsy 'mid their savage merriment,
Clanking these dreadful fetters in their ears.

   Clergyman. I will return at night.

Prisoner.   O leave me not.
For I am scarcely in my sober mind.
A thousand fiends are waiting to destroy me
Soon as you leave the cell, for innocence
Is found not proof against the pains of hell.
   Clergyman. I will bring your wife to visit you.
   Prisoner, (kneeling.)   O God
Of tender mercies, let thy countenance
Shine on that wretched one. Let this cell lie
Forsaken of thy presence—if thy will—
But, for His sake who died upon the cross,
Let heavenly sunshine fall into her soul!
Temper the wind to the shorn lamb that lies
Upon her breast in helpless infancy!
O! if our cottage could but rest in peace,
Here could I pass the remnant of my life
In lonely resignation to my fate.
Forsake not her and my sweet family.
   Clergyman. Man forsakes man—that melancholy word
Applieth not to gracious Providence.
   Prisoner. I am not then forsaken.
   Clergyman.   Fear it not!
Wrapt in the dark cloud of adversity,
Thou art indeed; but clouds are of the earth.
Lift up the eye of Faith, and thou wilt see
The clear blue sky of the untroubled heavens.
   Prisoner. My soul at once is calm'd—now let us pray.

THE CONVICT.

PART II.

___

SCENE I.

The morning of the day of execution—The young CLER-
GYMAN *and another* FRIEND *sitting beside the* PRI-
SONER, *who is asleep.*

Clergyman. He stirs as he would wake.
Friend.   List! list! he speaks!
Clergyman. A smile is on his face—a kindling smile.
Friend. Oh! when he wakes!
Clergyman.   Hearken—he speaks again.
Prisoner (in his sleep.) O my sweet Alice! 'Twas a
    dreadful dream!
Am I in truth awake? Come to my heart!
There—there—I feel thy breath—pure—pure—most
    pure.
Friend. What a deep sigh of overwhelming bliss!
Hell gapes for him when he awakes from heaven.

Clergyman. Will not the same benignant Providence
That blesseth now his sleep, uphold him falling
Into the shadow of death!

Prisoner. No tears my Alice!
Weep—weep no more! Where is our infant Alice?
Esther where art thou? Mary? My sweet twins!
—I dreamt that I had bid thee farewell Alice!
Why is that loving voice so slow to speak?
Hold me to thy bosom lest the curse return!
Why beats thy heart so....

Friend. Lo! his glazed eyes
Are open—but methinks he sees us not.

Prisoner. (*starting up.*) My family are swept off from
    the earth.
—I know not, in the darkness of my brain,
My dreams from waking thoughts nor these from dreams.
—Yes! yes! at once 'tis plain. O heaven of heavens!
Thou canst not be in all thy sanctity
A place so full of perfect blessedness,
As the bed where I was lying in my dream.

Clergyman. We have been praying for thee all the
    night.

Prisoner. What! my dear friends! good morning to
    you both.
Have I been sleeping long?

Clergyman. Since four o'clock,
And now 'tis almost eight.

Prisoner. Blest was that sleep

Beyond all human bliss! I was at home,
And Alice in my bosom·····Come my Friend,
You must not thus be overcome, this hour
Too awful is for tears. Look not on me
As on a son of anguish and despair,
But a Man, sorely stricken though he be,
Supported by the very power of Sorrow,
And Faith that comes a solemn comforter
Even hand in hand with death.

Clergyman. Most noble spirit!
Fitter art thou with that untroubled voice
To comfort us than to be comforted.

Prisoner. This cell hath taught me many a hidden
 thing.
I have become acquainted with my soul
Through midnight silence, and through lonely days
Silent as midnight. I have found therein
A well of waters undisturbed and deep,
Of sustenance, refreshment, and repose.

Clergyman. On earth nought may prevail o'er inno-
 cence.

Prisoner. One night, methought, a voice said in my
 cell,
" Despondency, and Anguish, and Despair
" Are falling on thee! curse thy God and die!"—
" Peace, Resignation, and Immortal Hope,"
A dewy voice replied. It was a dream.
But the good angel's voice was in my soul,

Most sweet when I awoke, and from that hour,
A heavenly calm hath never left my cell.

Friend. O must we part for ever from our Friend!
Is there no hope? The hour of agony
Is hastening on, and there is none to save!

Clergyman. Forgive his grief. 'Tis easier to resign
Ourselves unto our fate, than to endure
The sight of one we love about to die.

Prisoner. A little brook doth issue from the hill
Above Lea-side, and, ere it reaches us,
Its course is loud and rocky, crying still
As with a troubled voice. But o'er the green
That smiles beside our door it glideth on,
Just like a dream so soft and silently,
For ever cheerful and for ever calm.
Last night when you came here—I had been thinking
Of that sweet brook, and it appear'd to me
An emblem of my own much alter'd soul,
Lately so troubled, but now flowing on
In perfect calmness to eternity.

Friend. Thinking of Lea-side even unto the last.

Prisoner. Yes! I will think of it unto the last,
Of heaven and it by turns. There is no reason
Why it should be forgotten while I live.
I see it, like a picture on that wall,
In the silence of the morning, with its smoke,
Its new waked smoke slow wreathing up to heaven!

And from that heaven, where, through my Saviour's
    death,
I humbly hope to be, I will look down
On that one spot—Oh! sure the loveliest far
On the wide earth! too sweet! too beautiful!
Too blest to leave without a gush of tears.
—They will drive me past my own door to the scaffold?
    Friend. Such is the savage sentence.
    Prisoner.   It is well.
    Friend. We never will forsake you to the last—
But proudly sit beside you······
    Prisoner.   Sweet Lea-side!
And I will see my little farm again!
New-thatched with my own hand this very Spring—
All full of blossoms is my garden now,
And the sweet hum of bees!—Hush'd be the wheels
As o'er a depth of snow, when they pass by!
That Alice may not hear the fearful sound,
And rush out with my children in her arms.
    Clergyman. Fear not—she hath gone into her father's
    house.
    Prisoner. I thought our parting had been past. But
    no!
Souls cannot part though parting words be breathed,
With deep abandonment of earthly loves.
Had I not dreamt that heavenly dream last night
Perhaps it had been so—but in that dream
My human nature burst again to life,

And I think upon my widow as before
With love, grief, shame, dismay, and agony.

   Clergyman. I am the father, says our gracious God,
Of the orphan and the widow.

   Prisoner.   'Twas a pang!
A passing pang! *(going to the window)* It is a sunny
      day.
Methinks if I had any tears to shed,
That I could weep to see the fading world
So beautiful! How brightly wilt thou smile
O Sun, to-morrow when my eyes are dark!
O 'tis a blessed earth I leave behind!

                             [*A noise at the door.*]

   Friend. It is not yet the time!

   Jailor enters.   In half an hour
They will come to fetch the prisoner from his cell.

                                  [*Goes out.*]

   Friend. O scowling savage! What a heart of stone.

   Prisoner. I think he is less cruel than he seems.
Sometimes his face hath worn a look of pity,
And his voice soften'd; but his heart is blind
In ignorance, and harden'd by the sight
Of unrepentant wickedness, and sorrows
Which human sympathy would fail to cure.
He seem'd disturb'd—he feels all he can feel.

   Clergyman. Thou art indeed a Christian.

   Prisoner.   Death is near.
You know my heart, and will reveal it truly

To all who know my tale. The time will come
When innocence will vindicate itself,
And shame fall off my rising family
Like snow shaken from the budding trees in spring.
—They doubt not of their father's innocence?

Clergyman. Unshaken is the confidence of love
In hearts that know not sin—thy memory
Hallow'd by tribulation will endure......

Prisoner. Enough—enough. Here take this blessed
  book,
Which from my dying father I received,
And give it to my wife. Some farewell thoughts
I have dared to write beneath my children's names,
Recorded duly there soon as baptized.
And now I have no more to say to man.
Leave me alone a little while—and wait
In the open street, till I appear before you.

Friend. We fear to leave the cell—you look so pale!
As if about to faint.

Prisoner (holding out his hand with a smile.) My pulse
  is steady.

Clergyman. We leave thee to thy God!

SCENE II.

Inside of a cottage.—The prisoner's WIFE *sitting with her*
  FRIEND, *surrounded by her family.*

Wife. Speak to me! let my weeping children speak,
Although it be with sobs of agony.

Friend. See how composed your sweetest children sit
All round your knees! They weep, and sigh, and sob,
For piteous they and most compassionate.
But nature steals upon them in their grief,
And happy thoughts, in spite even of themselves,
Come o'er them—the glad light of infancy.
Mourn not for them—in little William's hand,
Although his heart be framed of love and pity,
Already see that play-thing! none need weep
For them a gracious God preserves in bliss.

Wife. 'Tis not on them I think—O God! O God!

Friend. He soon will be in Heaven.

Wife. A dreadful path
Must first be trod. O 'tis most horrible!

Friend. Since that last scene is present to your soul
I dare to speak of it. The face of death
More hideous seems to us who gaze upon it
Bent towards a friend we love, than to the wretch
Who sees the black frown fix'd upon himself.
The fears of fancy are most terrible,
But when the apprehended misery comes,
The spirit smiles to feel how bearable
The heaviest stroke of fate.

Wife. Thy kind voice seems
To speak of comfort, though the words are dark.
Misery's sick soul is slow to understand,
Yet I will listen, for that gentle voice
Brings of itself relief.

s

Friend.   Calm, unappall'd—
How many mount the scaffold! Even Guilt
Strong in repentance often standeth there
And quaketh not. And will not innocence
Victoriously from that most rueful place
Look o'er the grave—nor death's vain idle show
Have power to raise one beating in his heart?

   Wife. O what a dreadful night he must have past!

   Friend. Nay—fear it not—the night before they die,
Condemned men enjoy unbroken sleep,
By mercy sent to their resigned souls,
Calming and strengthening for the morrow's trial.
While we were weeping—his closed eyes were dry,
And his soul hush'd in deep forgetfulness.

   Wife. I feel as if I ne'er shall sleep again!
The look with which he flung his body down
On the stone-floor, when I was carried from him,
Will never pass away. O that sweet face
Was changed indeed by nature's agony,
Sunk, fallen, hollow, bloodless and convulsed!

   Friend. O strive to think on other prison-hours
When on your knees together, lost in prayer,
You seem'd two happy Beings offering up
Thanksgiving, rather than poor suppliants
Imploring resignation to your doom.

   Wife. No. I will think but of that desperate hour
When darkness fell between us, there to brood
Until we meet in heaven. Come near to me,

For I must tell thee how my husband look'd
When wicked men did tear those two asunder
Whom God, and love, and nature had united.

   Friend. O spare me—spare me—on yourself have
      pity,
And these soft-hearted ones—too apt to weep!

   Wife. Why should I fear to speak?

   Friend.   Your Infant wakes!
Here, take it to your breast—

   Wife.   Heed, heed it not.
—For hours we sat, and dreamt, and spoke, and wept,
Recall'd our happy life to memory,
From the hour we first met on yon sunny brae!
Our friendship, love, and marriage,—the sweet child
That came to bless our first delightful spring—
All our sweet children! not forgetting her
Who went so young to heaven. The Jailor came,
Or some one with a black and cruel countenance,
And changed at once our sorrow to despair.
We had not thought of parting—in the past
So buried were our hearts!—such images
Blinded our spirits with the tears of love,
And though we felt a dire calamity
Brought us together in that hideous cell,
We thought not what it was; till all at once,
The prison-door flew open, and they dragged me
Not shrieking—as perhaps I now do shriek—
But with a cold weight sickening at my heart

That in convulsions drown'd a thousand shrieks,
And brought at last a dark forgetfulness
Of my own sufferings, and my husband's doom.
Long streets seem'd passing slowly by my brain,
And fields and trees—until at once I knew
The faces of my weeping family,
And this my Father's house. A dreadful dream!
Yet could I wish to rave of it for ever!

[*Her eldest* DAUGHTER *steals up with a Book in her hand.*]

Daughter. Here is a book which little Mary Grieve,
(She who has wept as much for my poor Father
As if she were a sister of our own)
Gave me a week ago, a happy book,
Which lies below my pillow when I sleep.
Look at it Mother! 'tis the history
Of one repriev'd when just about to die.
I have read it till it seems a sad true tale
Of all my Father's woe—and when I read it
Ev'n on the darkest day, believe me Mother,
A gleam of sunshine falls upon the leaves,
Straight down from heaven! There is a picture—look!
Is it not like my Father's gentle face?

Wife. (*grasping the book.*) As sure as God is in heaven! it is the same!—.
His wife and children too with eyes and faces
Of mad delirious joy all fix'd on heaven!
And well they may—then and for evermore.

Daughter. I show'd it to our clergyman—he smil'd—
And laid his gentle hand upon my hair,
And with a low kind voice he bade me hope.
 Wife. He bade thee hope!
 Daughter.   Yes—and I thought he wept,
 Wife. He tried to comfort the sweet innocent!
 Daughter. Though I should see my father in the cart
Passing our very door......
 Wife.   Will he pass our door?
I will rush out and clasp him, and beseech
Kind heaven to let me die upon his breast.
          [*Goes towards the door.*]
I had forgot—we are not at Lea-side.
—Come to me little William—weep not child!
 Boy. O yesterday we saw a dreadful sight!
 Daughter. William—hold your peace.
 Wife.   What saw my little boy?
 Boy. We went last night to meet with Mary Grieve
Coming from school. And oh! upon the bridge
Two men were building up—I did not ask them—
They told me what it was—and we ran home
Fearing to look back.
 Wife.   O shut out the sun
That blinds my soul with its accursed light!
Close—close the shutters—that eternal darkness
May cover me and my poor family,
And the wild world with all its miseries
Be blank as if we all were in the grave.
          [*The shutters are closed.*]

Boy. Mother! let me come closer to your knees!
Wife. O let the light come in—this silent darkness
Is worse than light—light is but mockery—
But darkness is the haunted tomb of death
Which shuddering nature never may endure.
—I never thought thy face so sad before
As in that sudden light.—(*clock strikes.*)—What hour?
    what hour?
    Friend. Your husband's strife is o'er.
    Wife.   Praise be to God.
(*Falls on her knees.*) O Thou that art an angel in the
    sky,
Strengthen my soul that I on earth may cherish
Those whom thou lov'st—these infants round my feet.
    Friend. Such prayers go up to heaven—swifter than
    light.
    Wife. The body shall have Christian-burial!
I will away that no base hand disturb it.
What though it felt the cruel death of shame,
Is it not beautiful and fair to see,
As if he rested from the harvest-toil
In some cool shady place o'erhung with trees?
It shall be dress'd with flowers—a thousand times,
A thousand thousand times my lips will kiss it,
And when it is laid in the grave at last,
Oh! will not tears from many hundred eyes
Fall on the coffin, and a hundred tongues
Bless him th' unhappy—him the innocent?

—Methinks I can endure the daylight now.
                    [*She goes to the window.*]
O Lord! yon hill-side is quite black with people
All standing motionless—with heads uncover'd.
Are they gazing all on him? Alive? or dead?—
This is a sight to drive my soul to madness,
To blasphemy and disbelief in God!

 Friend. I thought the hour was past.

 Wife.   You knew it was not.
Upon the self-same side of that black mount
I saw a pious congregation sitting
Last summer's sacrament! and now they come
To enjoy an execution. Wretched things!
They little understand the words of Christ.

 Friend. It seems in truth most cruel—dreadful show
Of fixed faces! many a troubled soul
Is gazing there, yet loves the agony
It makes itself to suffer—turns away—
Then looks and shudders, and with cheeks as wan
And ghastly as the man about to die,
Waits for the hideous moment—greedily
Devouring every motion of his eyes
Now only bent to heaven.

 Wife.   O senseless wretches!
Thus tamely witnessing the guiltless die.
Rush down upon the scaffold—rend it—crush it
Into a thousand atoms—tear away
Th' accursed halter from his innocent neck,

And send him like a lark let loose to heaven,
Into the holy light of liberty.
—One hour delay the execution!
For from afar the words of mercy come—
I hear them on the wind—"Reprieve—Reprieve"—
O gazing multitude! look grim no more,
But shout until both earth and heaven reply
Salvation is at hand—Reprieve—Reprieve.

[*She rushes out into the air followed by her* FRIEND *and her children, who endeavour to restrain her in vain.*]

SCENE III.

A Field in the Country.—Labourers reposing.

The Master. Come Mary Macintyre—give us a song,
Then to our work again. Thou hast a voice
So sweet, that even the Linnet on the broom
Might take a lesson from thee.

SONG.

A bird in Spring had built her nest
  In a tuft o' flowres on a Castle-wa',
Whare saftly on her bonny breast,
  The dew and light o' heaven did fa'.

Amang the moss and silky hair
  Twa young anes lay in love thegither—
And oh! their yellow plumes were fair
  When glinting in the sunny weather.

Upon that Tower for many an hour
    Anither bird would sit and sing,
Or resting on that red wa-flow'r
    In sleep would fauld his gowden wing.

Ae morning at the break o' day
    I saw the nest a' pearl'd wi' dew,
That like a net of diamonds lay
    Aboon that flow'r o' freshest hue.

I could na see the bonnie Bird,
    She cower'd sae close upon her nest,
But that saft ither sang I heard
    That lull'd her and her brood to rest.

Sweet through the silent dawning rung
    The pleasure o' that lanely sang,
And the auld Tower again look'd young
    That psalm sae sweetly sail'd alang.

Mair sweetly breath'd the birchen grove
    That wav'd upon the Castle-Hill,
And a' the earth look'd fresh wi' love
    The moment that the sang was still!

At gloaming I cam back that way,
    But I miss'd the flower sae red and sweet,
And the nest whare thae twa birdies lay,
    Waes me! was herried at my feet.

I wud na weep for the dead wa-flower,
    Sweet birds! gin I kent whare ye were gane,

But the low has blacken'd the auld Mearns-Tower,
   And bluid is drapping frae ilka stane.

And he that herried the Lint-white's nest,
   And kill'd the auld birds wi' his sling,
He wud na' spare the chirping breast
   Nor the down upon the wee bit wing.

Master. It is an old traditionary song.
The Maxwells in a body from Hag-Castle
At midnight came, and burn'd the good Mearns-Tower,
With young Laird Stewart and his English Lady,
And their four pretty bairns. They burn'd them all.
The Lady's blood is still upon the stones
Of the west-corner. Many a blashing storm
Hath driven across them, yet they still are red.
'Tis two o'clock, come to our work again!

Young Man. Oh! I am sick at heart! this very moment,
Is my poor Master standing on the scaffold!
Go, go to work—I will kneel down and pray
For his departing soul.

                                [*Kneels down.*]

Master.   His hour is come.
Men, women, children, now all rush to see him
In his white death-clothes standing like a ghost!
Aye, lasses, ye may weep—yet will that crowd
Show many a female face—girls like yourselves
In their best gowns adorn'd for holiday,—

And wives that love their husbands—and even mothers
With infants in their arms. Confound their cruelty.
Enough of death there is in this wide world
Near each man's fireside, or his neighbour's house!
Why rush to see him in the open day-light
Standing with fear, and shame, and agony?

  Mary. Oh! on that sweet hill-side he often sat
Watching his young spring-lambs! and now even there
Is he about to die the death of shame!

  Master. Methinks I see the hill-side all alive,
With silent faces gazing steadfastly
On one poor single solitary wretch,
Who views not in the darkness of his trouble
One human face among the many thousands
All staring towards the scaffold! Some are there
Who have driven their carts with his unto the market,
Have shook hands with him meeting at the Fair,
Have in his very cottage been partakers
Of the homely fare which rev'rently he blessed,
Yea! who have seen his face in holier places,
And in the same seat been at worship with him,
Within the House of God. May God forgive them!

  Mary. He is not guilty.

  Master.   Every thing is dark.
Last in the company of the murder'd man—
Blood on his hands—a bloody knife concealed—
The coin found on him which the widow swore to—
His fears when apprehended—and the falsehoods

Which first he utter'd—all perplex my mind!
And then they say the murder'd body bled,
Soon as he touch'd it.—Let us to our work,
Poor people oft must work with heavy hearts.
—Oh! doth that sunshine smile as cheerfully
Upon Lea-side as o'er my happy fields!

[*The Scene changes to a little field commanding a view of the place of execution. Two* YOUNG MEN *looking towards it.*]

1*st Man.* I dare to look no longer.—What dost thou
  see?
2*d Man.* There is a stirring over all the crowd.
All heads are turn'd at once. O God of heaven!
There Francis Russel comes upon a cart,
For which a lane is open'd suddenly!
On, on it goes—and now it has arrived
At the scaffold foot.
  1*st Man.*   Say! dost thou see his face?
  2*d Man.* Paler than ashes.
  1*st Man (coming forward).* Let me have one look.
O what white cheeks! see, see—his upward eyes
Even at this distance have a ghastly glare.
I fear that he is guilty. Fear has bathed
In clammy dew his long lank raven hair.
His countenance seems convulsed—it is not paleness
That dims his cheeks—but a wild yellow hue
Like that of mortal sickness or of death.

Oh! what the soul can suffer, when the Devil
Sits on it, grimly laughing o'er his prey,
Like a carrion-bird beside some dying beast,
Croaking with hunger and ferocity.
[*He turns away.*]
  2d Man. He is standing on the scaffold—he looks
      round—
But does not speak—some one goes up to him—
He whispers in his ear—he kisses him—
He falls on his knees—now no one on the scaffold
But he and that old Wretch! a rope is hanging
Right over his head—and as my Maker liveth
That demon as he grasps it with his fingers
Hath laughter on his face.
  1st Man.   How look the crowd?
  2d Man. I saw them not—but now ten thousand
      faces
Are looking towards him with wide-open eyes!
Uncover'd every head—and all is silent
And motionless, as if 'twere all a dream.
  1st Man. Is he still praying?
  2d Man.   I can look no more,
For death and horror round his naked neck
Are gathering! Curse those lean and shrivell'd fingers
That calmly—slowly—and without a tremble—
Are binding unto agony and shame
One of God's creatures with a human soul.
—Hark! hark! a sudden shriek—a yell—a shout!

The whole crowd tosses like a stormy sea.
But oh! behold how still and motionless
That figure on the scaffold!
 1st Man.   What can it mean?
 2d Man. Perhaps with one soul all the crowd rise up
To rescue him from death.
 1st Man.   Let us away
And know what happens. Hark! another shout
That rends the silent sky. See hats are waved!
And every face is bright—deliverance
Is in that peal of joy—he shall not die.

   [*Scene changes to the place of execution.*]
 Sheriff. Bring the man up—and let us hear his story.
   [*A* Soldier *is dragged along by the crowd.*]
 Soldier. I am the murderer.
 One of the crowd.   Here is Stephen's watch—
The watch of the murder'd man—and his very purse—
Both found upon the villain.
 Sheriff.   'Tis strong proof.
—What have you got to say against this charge?
 Soldier. I robb'd and murder'd him—that's all—'tis
  true.
 One of the crowd. Just as the prisoner rose up from
  his knees,
This soldier at my side took out his watch,
And with a cruel and unchristian oath
Proclaim'd the hour, in laughing mockery.
My eye by chance fell on it—and the truth

Burst on my soul. I leapt upon the wretch,
And with a horrid cry he made confession
That he was the guilty man.
 Sheriff.   Scarce credible.
 Soldier. 'Tis true. Last night I saw the Evil-One
In human shape—as I sat among my comrades,
He stood close to my side—invisible
To all but me—and with a fiery eye
He then commanded me to go this day
And see the execution. So I came!
—And now behold the open gates of hell!
 Sheriff. The execution cannot thus proceed.
 Soldier. A little while—but yet a little while—
And I will come into the roaring pit
To dwell for ever with the damn'd!
 One of the crowd.   Mad—mad!
 Sheriff. Aye! 'tis the madness of despair and guilt.
Unhalter yon poor wretch—he must be carried
Back to his prison—till the truth appear.
 [*The* PRISONER's *wife, accompanied by her* FRIEND
  and children, rush through the crowd.]
 Wife. Come down—come down—my husband! from
  the scaffold.
—O Christ! art thou alive—or dead with fear!
Let me leap up with one bound to his side,
And strain him to my bosom till our souls
Are mix'd like rushing waters.

Dost hear thy Alice? Come down from the scaffold,
And walk upon the green and flowery earth
With me, thy wife, in everlasting joy!
  [*She tries to move forward, but falls down in a fainting-fit.*]
  One of the crowd. See—see his little daughter! how
    she tears
The covering from his eyes—unbinds the halter—
Leaps up to his bosom—and with sobs is kissing
His pale fix'd face. " I am thy daughter—Father!"
But there he stands—as lifeless as a stone—
Nor sees—nor feels—nor hears—his soul seems gone
Upon a dismal travel!
  [*The* Prisoner *is led down from the scaffold, with his daughter held unconsciously in his arms.*]
  Prisoner. Must this wild dream be all dream't o'er
    again!
Who put this little Child into my arms? My wife
Lying dead!—Thy judgments heaven! are terrible.
  The Clergyman. Look up—this world is shining out
    once more
In welcome to thy soul recalled from death.
  Prisoner. Oh! might that be—but this is not a dream
From which I may awake.—What, what has happened?
  Clergyman. The murderer is discovered.
  [*The prisoner falls on his knees, and his wife, who has recovered, goes and kneels by his side.*]

Clergyman. Crowd not so round them—let the glad
  fresh air
Enter into their souls.
 Prisoner. Alice! one word!
Let me hear thy voice assuring me of life.
Ah me! that soft cheek brings me by its touch
From the black, dizzy, roaring brink of death,
At once into the heart of happiness!
—Gasping with gratitude! she cannot speak.
 Wife. I never shall smile more—but all my days
Walk with still footsteps, and with humble eyes,
An everlasting hymn within my soul
To the great God of Mercy!
 Prisoner (starting up). O thou bright angel with that
  golden hair,
Scattering thy smiles like sunshine through the light,
Art thou my own sweet Daughter! Come, my Child
Come dancing on into thy Father's soul!
Come with those big tears sparkling on thy cheeks,
And let me drink them with a thousand kisses.
—That laugh hath fill'd the silent world with joy!
 Child. This night I will sit upon your knees once
  more,—
And oh! if ever I offend my Father!....
No—never,—never!—All our Cottage stands
Just as you left it—the old oaken chair

T

Will be fill'd to-night,—and our sweet hearth will
    burn
As it used to do—upon my Father's face!
—I too will pray—for though a little Child,
God now will hear my prayers!

   Prisoner (looking round).   The fields and hills
Have now return'd into their usual shape,
And all the sunny earth seems beautiful
As in my boyish days!——Oh! tell me—tell me—
Did I disgrace myself by abject fear
On the way from prison to yon hideous place?

   Clergyman. No—thou wert calm......
   Prisoner.   My friend—O say not so.
For from the moment that I left the prison
Blind horror seized me—and I thought the earth
Was reddening round me from the bloody sky.
I recollect some faces in the cart
Glimmering! and something like a bridge we past
Over a deep glen fill'd with raging thunder!
Then all was hush'd—and rose the voice of psalms
Doleful and wild! when suddenly I stood
In the fixed gazing of a million eyes,
And the feeling of my own identity
Came like a flash of lightning through my heart.

  Crowd. Huzza! huzza! the guiltless is set free!
Lea-side to-night, and all its happy fields,

Shall shine as bright as in the gladsome day.
For we will kindle on yon little green
A bonfire that shall set the heavens on flame,
And send up sparkling to the far-off stars
Beams like themselves—bright with deliverance.
Huzza! huzza! The guiltless is set free!
[The scene closes.]

The preceding scenes formed the conclusion of a dramatic poem, of which the first part was accidentally destroyed. I had narrated the circumstances which attached suspicion of the crime of murder to an innocent man—his terror and dismay on the charge being made against him—his trial and conviction—and the grief and misery of his family. The scenes now published must therefore, I feel, be perused with less interest, than if the reader had been previously made to sympathise keenly with the character and situation of the convict and his family.

THE SISTERS.

Sweet Creature! issuing like a dream
So softly from that wood!
—She glideth on a sunny gleam—
In youth in innocence so bright,
She lendeth lustre to day-light,
And life to solitude!
O'er all her face a radiance fair
That seemeth to be native there!
No transient smile, no burst of joy
Which time or sorrow may destroy,
A soul-breathed calm that ne'er may cease!
The spirit of eternal peace!
The sunshine may forsake the sky,
But the blue depths of ether lie
In steadfast meek serenity.
Onward she walks—with that pure face
Shedding around its gladdening grace—
Those cloudless eyes of tenderest blue
Sparkling through a tearlike dew—

THE SISTERS.

That golden hair that floats in air
Fine as the glittering gossamer—
That motion dancing o'er the earth
Without an aim—in very mirth—
That lark-like song whose strengthening measure
Is soaring through the air of pleasure—
—Is she not like the innocent Morn?
When from the slow-unfolding arms
Of Night, she starts in all her charms,
And o'er the glorious earth is borne,
With orient pearls beneath her feet,—
All round her, music warbling sweet,
And o'er her head the fulgent skies
In the fresh light of Paradise.

Lo! Sadness by the side of Joy!
—With raven tresses on her brow
Braided o'er that glimpse of snow—
O'er her bosom stray locks spread
As if by grief dishevelled—
Unsparkling eyes where smiles appear
More mournful far than many a tear—
Voice most gentle, sad, and slow,
Whose happiest tones still breathe of woe—
As in our ancient Scottish airs,
Even joy the sound of sorrow wears—
Motion like a cloud that goes
From deep to more profound repose—

Seems she not in pensive light
Image of the falling night?
—Still survive faint gleams of day,
But all sinking to decay—
There is almost mirth and gladness,
Temper'd soft with peace and sadness—
Sound comes from the stream and hill,
But the darkening world is still—
The heavens above are bright and holy,
Most beautiful—most melancholy—
And gazing with suspended breath,
We dream of grief—decay—and death!

THE FAREWELL AND RETURN.

I WENT where two dear friends did dwell,
Husband and Wife—to bid farewell,
Before I left my peaceful home,
Alone through distant lands to roam.
I found them by their sparkling hearth,
In perfect love and inward mirth—
Through virtue happy in themselves,
And sporting with four beauteous Elves,
Who, like the tender flowers of Spring
Mov'd by the zephyr's lightest wing,
Danced here and there in playful guise,
With sunny heads and laughing eyes,
With song of joy and wanton shout—
A happy—restless—maddening rout!

They look unto the opening door,
And all their noisy mirth is o'er!
To graveness sink their wanton wiles,
And blushes hide their struggling smiles.

Quick to their mother's lap they run,
As trembling to be look'd upon—
There half-delighted—half-afraid,
They hide, then slowly raise the head—
And venture thus to look at me
With sweet restraint and bashful glee,
Till the dear child I love the best
With downcast look steals from the rest,
And with an infant's blessed art
Twines her white arms around my heart.

And now the stir—the noise revive!
The little cottage seems alive,
As if a new-awaken'd soul
Like light were gladdening through the whole.
The happy parents smile to see
Their Mary lisping on my knee
With bolder look and freer tone,
As if she felt that seat her own.
While oft her gamesome brothers tried
To win from my protecting side
The little truant maid away,
By taunting jibe and novel play.
But vain both jibe and play to move
An infant's heart when touch'd with love!

Soon evening brings the hour of rest—
And Mary on my loving breast

THE FAREWELL AND RETURN.

Hath fallen asleep! so not to wake
The blessed babe, I gently take
Her guiltless bosom soft and fair,
Unto her bed—and breathe a prayer
That all her future life be spent
Happy as she is innocent!
Near me her joyful parents stand,
Bless me by name and press my hand—
Their mingling tones my spirit meet,
Though always kind now doubly sweet—
A golden chain in concord mild
Links closely Parents—Friend and Child.

Years past along—and lo! once more
I stand beside that cottage-door;—
The hour in which I went away
Seems but the eve of yesterday.
Motionless there I linger long,
O'erpower'd with a tumultuous throng
Of memories, fancies, hopes, and fears,
Sinkings of heart, sighs, smiles, and tears.
No cause had I for mournful thought,
Yet in my beating heart there wrought
A dread of something undefined!
While like the hollow midnight wind,
A voice fell sullen on my ear,
"Think not to find your Mary here!"

A dreary stillness reign'd around
Deep as the hush of burial-ground,
As if all life were banish'd thence
By breath of noisome pestilence.
Not so—I met a ghastly man
With haggard eyes and visage wan;
In his dim looks so charg'd with woe
My dearest friend I scarce could know.
One moment's pause—then did he fall
Upon my neck—and told me all!
That she my darling girl was dead,
And by his own hands newly laid
Spotless within her spotless shroud—
His voice here died—he wept aloud.

Vainly his tortur'd soul I cheer'd—
When lo! his wretched Wife appear'd,
Unlike that Wife when last we parted,
Then deeply blest—now broken-hearted.
She gaz'd on me with eye-balls wild,
And shriek'd the name of her dead Child;
And with convulsive sobs opprest
She fainted on her Husband's breast!
The memory of that happy night
Came o'er her like a sudden blight!
Those gentle looks—those melting smiles—
Those happy shouts—those wanton wiles—

That dreaming face upon its bed—
—Now lying there, pale, cold, and dead!

Ah me! beneath a beauteous sky
The Fairy-land of peace doth lie,
Through which united Spirits stray
Companions on the destin'd way
That leads to everlasting life!
Yet oft that darkening sky is rife
With thunder-bearing clouds! they fade—
And heaven's blue depths again display'd
Seem steep'd in quiet more profound!
—I walk'd unto the burial-ground,
Where that delightful Child doth rest—
There both her Parents deeply blest!
Methought I saw their souls rejoice,
Listening in heaven that Seraph's voice.

THE END.

Printed by George Ramsay and Co.
Edinburgh, 1816.

THE FAREWELL AND RETURN.

On Monday the 4th of December was Published,

Handsomely printed in Quarto, with Fifteen Plates, engraved (from Original Drawings) by the First Artists of London and Edinburgh,

Ah me! how pleas'd I am to know,

The FAREWELL!!!!!!!!! PART FIRST.

Through which untied Spirits stray

Companions on the dark'n'd w y

That....................

Yet on I our darkening way.......

SUPPLEMENT

With thunder-bellying cars , l .

And heaven's blue depths up........

OF THE

FOURTH AND FIFTH EDITIONS

—I walk'd unto the lay...........

Where that dolyphid- a l.tle cloth mil—

ENCYCLOPÆDIA BRITANNICA.

Methought I saw their souls , lol .

Lulapping in barren thus brough. , r

EDINBURGH:

PRINTED FOR ARCHIBALD CONSTABLE AND CO. SUCCESSORS

GALE AND FENNER, LONDON; THOMAS WILSON AND SONS,

YORK; ROBINSON, SON, AND HOLDSWORTH, LEEDS; JOHN

FOGGONS, HULL; AND JOHN DUMMING, DUBLIN.

THE END.

The Encyclopædia Britannica forms a General Dictionary

EDINBURGH, JANUARY 1816.

On Monday the 4th of December was Published,

Handsomely printed in Quarto, with Fifteen Plates, engraved (from Original Drawings) by the First Artists of London and Edinburgh,

PRICE L. 1, 5s. BOARDS,

VOLUME FIRST, PART FIRST,

OF

SUPPLEMENT

TO THE

FOURTH AND FIFTH EDITIONS

OF THE

ENCYCLOPÆDIA BRITANNICA.

EDINBURGH:
PRINTED FOR ARCHIBALD CONSTABLE AND CO. EDINBURGH; GALE AND FENNER, LONDON; THOMAS WILSON AND SONS, YORK; ROBINSON, SON, AND HOLDSWORTH, LEEDS; JOHN RODFORD, HULL; AND JOHN CUMMING, DUBLIN.

THE ENCYCLOPÆDIA BRITANNICA forms a General Dictionary, not only of Arts and Sciences, but of every branch of Human Knowledge. Its Plan has received the decided approbation of the most competent judges, particularly for its superior method of arrangement in regard to the Sciences; and the publication of

Five extensive Editions must be allowed to afford a very satisfactory proof of the favourable opinion of the Public at large.

The *Fifth* Edition, which contains a greatly improved set of Engravings, has just been completed in Twenty Volumes Quarto; and it is the object of the present Work, To supply all material omissions—to continue the Historical and Biographical, as well as the Geographical and Statistical information to the present times—and to exhibit the Arts and Sciences in their latest state of improvement. As the *Fifth* was reprinted without any material variation from the *Fourth* Edition, this SUPPLEMENT will of course be equally applicable to both; but though more immediately connected with these Two Editions, it must also prove a valuable sequel to the *Third*.

The utility of such an addition, to a Work in so many hands, as the ENCYCLOPÆDIA BRITANNICA, must indeed appear abundantly obvious; but the Publishers beg farther to mention, that this SUPPLEMENT is arranged upon a Plan, by which it will, within *itself*, afford a comprehensive view of the progress and present state of every department of Human Knowledge.

It will consist of Five Volumes, similar in size to those of the principal Work, and will be illustrated with numerous Engravings, executed in the best style of the art. The publication will proceed by *Parts*, or *Half Volumes*, to follow each other at as short intervals as the nature of the undertaking will permit.

To the first Half Volume there is prefixed a Dissertation, exhibiting a general view of the progress of *Metaphysical, Ethical,* and *Political Philosophy*, since the revival of Letters in Europe, by Mr DUGALD STEWART; and the second Volume will be prefaced with a similar view of the progress of *Mathematical* and *Physical Science*, by PROFESSOR PLAYFAIR.

Encyclopædia Britannica.

The Work will be edited by MACVEY NAPIER, Esq. F.R.S.E.; and the following Gentlemen have engaged to honour it with their co-operation:

Reverend ARCHIBALD ALISON, LL.B. F.R.S. L. & E.
JOHN AIKEN, M.D. F.L.S.
THOMAS ALLAN, Esq. F.R.S. L. and E.
JOHN BARROW, Esq. F.R.S. one of the Secretaries of the Admiralty.
WILL. THO. BRANDE, F.R.S. L. & E. Professor of Chemistry to the Royal Institution of London.
H. D. BLAINVILLE, M.D. Professor of Zoology and Comparative Anatomy, Paris.
Mr DAVID BUCHANAN.
WILLIAM ARCHIBALD CADELL, Esq. F.R.S. L. & E.
Mr ALEXANDER CHALMERS, F.S.A.
JOHN COLQUHOUN, Esq. Advocate.
Reverend GEORGE COOK, D.D.
ANDREW DUNCAN, Junior, M.D. F.R.S.E. Professor of Medical Jurisprudence in the University of Edinburgh.
JOHN GRAHAM DALYELL, Esq. Advocate.
JOHN DUNLOP, Esq. Advocate.
DANIEL ELLIS, Esq. F.R.S.E.
WILLIAM FERGUSON, M.D. Inspector of Hospitals to the Forces.
Mr FAREY, Jun. Draughtsman, London.
Reverend JOHN FLEMING, D.D. F.R.S.E.
JAMES GLASSFORD, Esq. Advocate.
JOHN GORDON, M.D. F.R.S.E. Lecturer on Anatomy and Physiology.
JAMES HORSBURGH, Esq. F.R.S. Hydrographer to the East India Company.
ALEXANDER HENDERSON, M.D. London.
ALEXANDER IRVINE, Esq. F.R.S.E. Advocate, Professor of Civil Law in the University of Edinburgh.
JAMES IVORY, A.M. F.R.S. Member of the Royal Society of Gottingen.
FRANCIS JEFFREY, Esq.
ROBERT JAMESON, F.R.S.E. Professor of Natural History in the University of Edinburgh.
CHARLES KÖENIG, Esq. F.R.S.—L.S. Mineralogist to the British Museum.

JOHN LESLIE, F.R.S.E. Professor of Mathematics in the University of Edinburgh.
STEPHEN LEE, Esq. F.R.S. London.
WILLIAM ELFORD LEACH, M.D. F.L.S. Zoologist to the British Museum.
WILLIAM LAWRENCE, Esq. F.R.S. Surgeon, London.
JOSEPH LOWE, Esq.
W. LOWRY, F.R.S. London.
CHARLES MACKENZIE, Esq. F.R.S.—L.S.
ROBERT MUSCHET, Esq. Royal Mint, London.
JAMES MILL, Esq. London.
JOSHUA MILNE, Esq. Actuary to the Sun Life Assurance Society.
Reverend ROBERT MOREHEAD, A.M. late of Bal. Col. Oxford.
HUGH MURRAY, Esq. F.R.S.E.
JOHN PLAYFAIR, F.R.S.L. and E. Professor of Natural Philosophy in the University of Edinburgh.
JAMES PILLANS, F.R.S.E. Rector of the High School, Edinburgh.
JAMES COWLES PRITCHARD, M.D. F.L.S.
PETER M. ROGET, M.D. F.R.S. London.
WALTER SCOTT, Esq.
Sir JAMES EDWARD SMITH, M.D. F.R.S. President of the Linnæan Society.
HENRY SALT, Esq. F.R.S.—L.S.
Mr SYLVESTER, Derby.
Mr STODDART, London.
WILLIAM STEVENSON, Esq. London.
THOMAS THOMSON, M.D. F.R.S. L. and E.
JOHN TAYLOR, Esq. Civil Engineer, London.
Rev. WILLIAM TURNER, Newcastle.
WILLIAM WALLACE, F.R.S.E. one of the Professors of Mathematics, Royal Military College, Sandhurst.

The Publishers, in conclusion, cannot but hope, that this Work holds out recommendations of such a kind, as to render it highly acceptable, not only to those who possess copies of the Encyclopædia Britannica, but to the Public at large.

₄ The *Second* Part of Vol. I., illustrated with upwards of Twenty Plates, will be Published in March.

CPSIA information can be obtained
at www.ICGtesting.com
Printed in the USA
BVHW041308030120
568503BV00007B/26/P

9 780342 809660